Training Manual
Levels I & II

Adrian Campbell, PhD

Illustrations by
Tricia Dietrich & Shawn Palmer

Copyright 2024 by Adrian Campbell, PhD

Cover and internal design by Adrian Campbell, PhD

All rights reserved. No part of this book may be reproduced in any form or by any electronic or mechanical means including information storage and retrieval systems - except in the case of brief quotations embodied in critical articles or reviews - without permission in writing from Adrian Campbell, PhD.

Published by Adrian Campbell, PhD
www.EnergeticPsyche.com

Table of Contents

Introduction 4

Chapter 1: Getting to Know the Energetic Body 8

    Everything Is Energy Meditation 10

    Everything is Energy 16

    The Aura 16

    The Chakra System 20

    Working with the Energetic Body 22

    Connecting with Your Chakra System 24

Chapter 2: Understanding Reiki Energy Healing 31

    What is Energy Healing? 32

    Reiki Energy Healing 33

    Reiki Masters & Attunements 34

Chapter 3: Energy Healing Techniques 39

    Energy Healing & its Uses 40

    Working with Reiki 41

    Getting the Flow Going 43

    FAQs About Working with Reiki 44

    Self-Sessions 50

    Intuitive Self-Session 50

    Standard Self-Session Hand Placements 52

    Alternative Sessions and Hand Placements 56

    Guided Intuitive Self-Session Meditation 57

Chapter 4: The Healing Power of Crystals 65
The Healing Power of Crystals 67
Using Reiki with Crystals 68
Creating Crystal "Healing Bundles" 69

Chapter 5: Using Reiki Energy with Others 72
Tending to the Wellness of Others 75
Standard hand placements for others 77
Intuitive Sessions for others 81

Chapter 6: Usui Holy Fire Reiki Level II Symbols 84
Using Reiki Symbols 86
The Power Symbol 87
The Mental & Emotional Healing Symbol 88
The Distance Healing Symbol 88

Chapter 7: Working with Reiki in Everyday Life 93
Elements of a Complete Level II Reiki Session 94
Developing Your Own Style 95
Working with Animals 95
Additional Uses for Reiki... 97
Creating Crystal Grids 101
Using Reiki in Co-creation & Manifestation 104

Chapter 8: Doing Business as a Reiki Practitioner 111
Spiritual Practice as a Business? 112
Charging for Sessions 114
Tools of the Trade 115

Finding a Practice Space 116

Websites, Marketing, etc. 117

Licenses, Taxes, & Insurance 118

The Reiki Ideals 120

Introduction

In 2010, I got a job working in the power generation industry, building on a career that started in the military and included work in the semi-conductor and geophysics industries. I worked 10+ hour days, sometimes six days a week, in an environment where nothing less than perfection was tolerated. Tired doesn't even come close to what I was, I was exhausted. But I was so used to life that way that anything else was foreign. Everyone around me lived and worked in the same way, it was expected of me, so I just kept doing it, until I couldn't.

In January of 2011, I began to experience headaches that would start across my brow and migrate to the back of my head, shooting stabbing pain into the bottom of my skull. I went to doctor after doctor who all incorrectly told me they were migraines. After ten months I had been prescribed multiple migraine medications that had no effect, had started to get spots in my vision, and was dealing with severe light sensitivity. I had such a high level of pain that I was prescribed an anti-inflammatory, opioids for pain, and a muscle relaxer, all of which I took daily, and yet it only took the edge off. I didn't know who I was anymore. I was angry all the time, lashed out at others, and basically split my time between work and home, where I would close all the blinds and lie on my couch drugged out, covered in heating pads, with my eyes closed most nights. I had started to lose hope that I would ever have a life worth living again.

By the end of the year, I was finally able to get into a neurologist who diagnosed me with Occipital Neuralgia and attributed it to the amount of stress I experienced at work. He referred me to the Pain Clinic where I after a few terrible treatments, extremely painful nerve block injections into the head and neck, I was told I would need to quit my job and continue with the injections every two weeks for the foreseeable future. WHAT?! No way. I refused to believe this was now my life. At this point, I went back to my neurologist and threw a fit like a two-year-old, screaming and crying about how this was all bullshit and there had to be a better way! He very flippantly told me, "Well, you can try acupuncture I guess", and that one statement changed my entire life.

I started acupuncture the next week with Mia Chou, the owner of Pacific Acupuncture in Dana Point, CA. We started with bi-weekly sessions and within one month of treatment I was off all the drugs and well on my way to being pain free. I couldn't believe it! Like really, I was like whaaaa?! How is this possible?

So being the nerdy girl I am, I started researching all kinds of alternative methods of wellness. As the years went by, I tried out Mindfulness-Based Stress Reduction (MBSR) meditation, Reiki, Crystal Healing, Hot Yoga, Gentle Yoga, Yin Yoga, haha allll the yogas! I also dabbled in sound healing, breathwork, somatic body work, massage, dream work, and more. And though I enjoyed most of it, and still do, Reiki was the one thing that I really connected to no matter what, the one thing that felt like it held the door open to all kinds of healing opportunities for me, and so I decided to get certified so I could give myself regular sessions.

Now, I kid you not, I never intended to give Reiki to another living soul, let alone teach it, or write this book, but once the energy lit up in my hands it was like I had just been given the best gift I could ever imagine. I will never forget feeling the energy flow through my hands right after my Level I attunement, just staring at it in amazement. Like oh my god, how freaking cool! And in that moment, I knew there was no way I was keeping this to myself.

I started small, giving Reiki sessions to friends and family, and after a bit I started offering Reiki sessions to private clients and even in Mia's acupuncture clinic (by this point we were basically besties). As time went by, my intuitive gifts began to grow and I wanted to be able to work with people in a deeper way. I started with a 12month long certified coaching program, and decided I needed more, so I went to grad school. All these years later I now have a PhD in Somatic Depth Psychology and a beautifully diverse practice that includes Reiki, Coaching, Dreamwork, Somatic Mindfulness and more. I work with some of the most amazing people and am so grateful every day for the work I am able to do in the world.

When I first began teaching Reiki in 2014, and for many years afterwards, I used the guidance and materials from a well establish Reiki training center, the one I had been trained through. But, as time went by and my own practice evolved, I found that teaching from their materials became more challenging, and I was consistently adding more and more supplemental information to be able to share Reiki in a way that felt true to who I was and what I had to offer my students. Eventually I knew it was time to create my own book, and so here we are.

This book is primarily designed to be used during a Reiki I/II certification course, or by someone who has already been certified. Sure, there is a lot of great info for just about anyone, but without the attunement you receive during the certification you won't be able to make the most of what is presented. If you are interested in learning Reiki please feel free to check out my scheduled classes on www.EnergeticPsyche.com or search for another instructor in your local area. Classes are available both in-person and online, and by a variety of different teachers. Who you choose to learn Reiki from is a personal decision and I highly recommend you take a look at a few offerings, talk with the teachers, maybe even take the time to meet them or get a session from them so that you can make the choice that is best for you. At the end of the day Spirit will guide you to where you belong, and I know in my heart you will find who you are meant to be with. I wish you all the very best this life has to offer.

with Love & Light, Adrian

What led you to learn Reiki?

Chapter 1

Everything Is Energy Meditation

We'll begin this section with a meditation to help us move inward towards the spark that connects us all.

(Feel free to record yourself reciting this meditation
and then listen to it as many times as you'd like.)

Begin by sitting or lying down.
I invite you to close your eyes or lower your gaze.

Allow your body to flex or stretch in any way that it needs. Maybe roll your head from side to side, perhaps forward and backward... Wiggle and stretch your fingers or toes... Roll your wrists in circles, maybe your shoulders, forwards and then backwards... Take a few moments to allow any physical energy to find release through subtle movement... when you are ready, settle into a position that you will find comfortable for the duration of the meditation.

Now I'll invite you to take a few deep breaths. Breathing in, nice and deep, expanding the lungs, the belly... and then exhaling out every last bit of air from your lungs. Breath in again, nice deep breath, again expanding the lungs, the belly, really filling yourself all the way up, and then exhaling out every last bit of air, feeling your navel draw in towards the spine, until you breathe in again, one last deep breath, expanding, filling, and then one final exhale through the mouth, letting it all go

Now release any control of the breath and return to your natural breathing.

...continued

Everything Is Energy Meditation (cont.)

Imagine within you, there is a spark.

This is the spark that lives within us all, that fuels us, that keeps us up and moving, this is the spark of life. Find this spark within you, deep within your being, within your heart, and allow all of your attention to focus on this spark…

Notice that this spark is not stagnant, but alive. Watch it as it glows, pulses, shifts in size and strength… notice that the glow from this spark does not end at the edges of it's source, but rather, the glow extends… follow the glow of this spark, the warm golden glow of this spark as it extends out throughout your body… feeling the glow move out from the chest, warming you as it goes… across the abdomen… down through the hips and the legs… grounding you to the earth… flowing up into the neck and shoulders… down the arms, and into the fingers… up and along the jaw, over the cheeks, ears, eyes, and forehead… finding it's way to the crown of your head and stretching up and outward, connecting you to all that is above and beyond… be with this feeling for a few moments, allowing the warmth of this glow to wash over your entire being, feeling yourself safely grounded to the earth beneath you and connected to all that is above.

…continued

Everything Is Energy Meditation (cont.)

Remembering to breathe... allowing this golden glow to completely envelop you... feeling yourself in your body, your body enveloped by this beautiful glow... keeping your eyes closed, allow yourself to once again move any part of your body that would like to move, gently flexing, rolling, stretching, all while feeling yourself emanating with this beautiful golden glow. Allow yourself to inwardly watch the energy shift as you begin to move your body. How does it flex along with you? How does it shift and change in tandem with your movement? Spend some time in this space, being in movement with the energy of the spark.

When you are ready I invite you to slowly and gently crack open your eyelids, but only a bit... allow yourself to imagine you see this glow surrounding every inch of your body. Extending out from your skin into the world around you... what does it look like? How does it feel? Does it shift as you wiggle your fingers? Move your arms? Spend a few moments here in this space.

Now I invite you to slowly open your eyes fully and take a few moments to reflect on your experience.

Everything is Energy

We are energy, the animals and plants around us are energy. Even the inanimate objects that we observe, touch, and use on a daily basis are energy. We are all made up of atoms, held together by varying frequencies which determine what shape and form we will take.

And just like the spark of energy within you that we just experienced together, these energies are not stagnant, they are not isolated, they are not alone. We are all connected to one another, influence one another, and shape the daily reality that we get to experience.

What makes living beings different is the addition of a special type of energy, called life force energy. This energy is known across the world by different names, such as *Chi, Ki,* or *Prana*, to name a few. All of these terms describe a vital energy, which when low or restricted makes one more vulnerable to illness or injury. It is through energy healing practices, when intention is directed in a way that shifts frequency, we are able to help ensure this vital life force energy flows freely throughout our energetic bodies.

The Aura

As you experienced in the meditation, our life force energy is not contained by our physical body. Our energy extends out beyond our skin and into the world around us. It is an extension of ourselves, containing ripples, scars, and spots, just as our physical body does.

The size, shape and color can differ from hour to hour, or day to day, depending on how we feel based off experiences both past and present. Though, it is widely believed that we each have an underlying color with us from birth, that represents our foundational traits.

What I have found in my studies and practice is that when we feel safe and loved, when we are happy and excited, our auras tend to be big and bright, extending up to 10ft or more from our bodies. However, when one is sick, injured, or sad and perhaps not wanting to engage with the world, the aura is pulled in close to the body, extending maybe half an inch, if at all. Remember the aura is an extension of the self and reacts to our experiences like the physical body might.

The aura is the energetic manifestation of your thoughts, feelings, and beliefs, both conscious and unconscious. It is affected by what you experience, just as much as the mind and central nervous system. It is often how we first interact with the world around us, how we pick up and give off *vibes*. It is our auras that allow us to *feel* the energy in a room based on the energetic connections we share. Unfortunately, because we typically aren't aware of our auras, we don't pay them enough attention.

Think for a moment about how your body responds when you feel sad or when you are sick?

What about when you are happy or excited?

What shapes does it take?

"As you transform yourself, you transform the world"

~ Anodea Judith ~

The Chakra System

The chakra system is the metaphorical bridge between consciousness and matter. It is a part of our energetic body, and it affects our physical being (breathing, heart rate, and metabolism) just as emotions do.

The status of our chakra system directly affects the way we receive and interpret information, changing how we interact with the world.

Becoming more familiar with your system, the way you move and hold energy, will help you improve the health of your chakra system and your life overall.

There are seven major chakras, each of which represents a specific type of energy.

1	Root/Base	Survival/Grounding/Prosperity
2	Sacral	Emotions/Sexuality/Family
3	Solar Plexus	Power/Autonomy/Will
4	Heart	Compassion/Self Love
5	Throat	Self-Expression/Communication
6	Brow/Third Eye	Intuition/ Creativity
7	Crown	Consciousness/Spirit

Too often the chakras are viewed as discrete components which can be worked with individually, but this cannot be further from the truth. All the chakras work together in a holistic manner to maintain balance throughout your energetic system. When one chakra is out of balance, the entire system is affected.

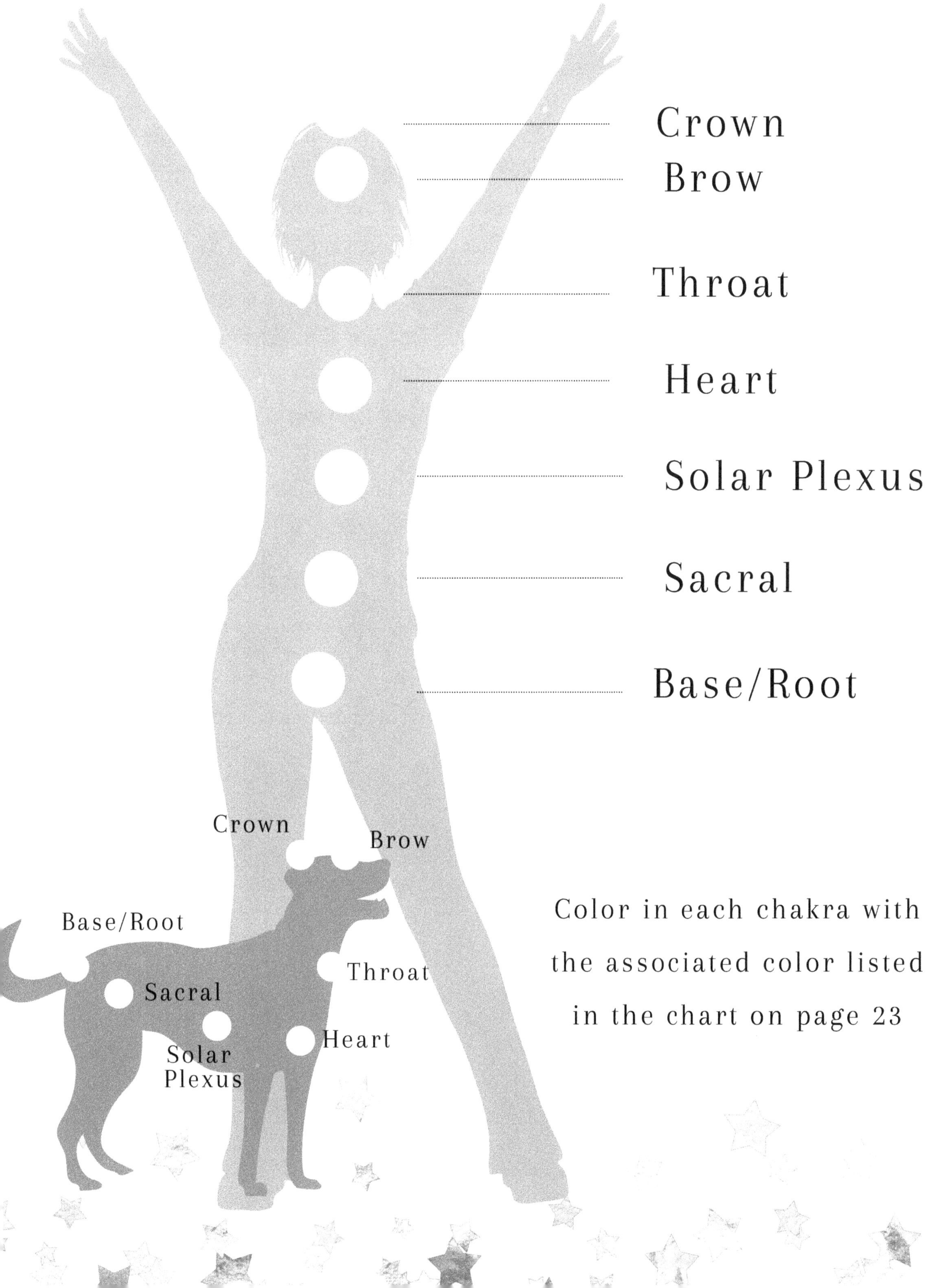

Crown

Brow

Throat

Heart

Solar Plexus

Sacral

Base/Root

Crown

Brow

Base/Root

Throat

Sacral

Heart

Solar Plexus

Color in each chakra with the associated color listed in the chart on page 23

The lower half of the system (chakras 1-3) focus on the physical realties of our existence, and the upper half of the system (chakras 5-7) focus on more ethereal and imaginative states. Chakra 4 connects the upper and lower halves of the system, putting love and compassion at the center of all things.

It is important that neither the upper nor lower half of the system is given preference, but rather, one should strive to bring the entire system into balance.

Working with the Energetic Body

There are multiple ways to heal energetic imbalances, as the chakra system maps onto both the mind and body, it can be accessed by both.

The chart on the next page has a few specific ways to work with each chakra. None is better than the other, but rather I implore you to listen to your intuition and go with what feels right for you.

Feel free to circle anything that pops out to you, or underline things that you know have worked for you in the past.

#	Name	Color	Crystal	Essential Oil	Nutrition	Activity
1	Root/Base	Red	Hematite, Bloodstone, Red Jasper, Carnelian, Garnet	Cedarwood, Patchouli, Vetiver, Spruce	Red foods – apples, raspberries, kidney beans, tomatoes, strawberries, pepper, beets	Earthing, dancing to a strong beat, drumming, being in nature
2	Sacral	Orange	Red and brown aventurine, red garnet, red jasper, carnelian	Orange, neroli, jasmine, rosewood, clary sage	Almonds, papaya, passion fruit, pumpkin, orange, coconut	Being in water, creative activities, dancing to fluid music
3	Solar Plexus	Yellow	Topaz, citrine, amber, tiger's eye	Lemongrass, fennel, coriander, lime, myrrh, lemon	Yellow foods – corn, squash, pineapples, peppers, brown rice, oats, ginger, turmeric	Affirmations to boost confidence, "baby step" challenges, warrior yoga poses, laugh
4	Heart	Green	Malachite, jade, green tourmaline, emerald, peridot	Ylang ylang, rose, jasmine, pine, rosewood	Green foods – spinach, kale, chard, lettuce	Loving Kindness Meditation, volunteer, gratitude practices
5	Throat	Turquoise	Turquoise, blue agate, lapis, aquamarine, sodalite	Rosemary, lime, sage, cedarwood, champa	Blue foods – currants, blackberries, blueberries, dragon fruit, kelp, wheatgrass, mushrooms	Singing, repeating mantras, chanting, journaling, vow of silence
6	Brow	Indigo	Lapis, indigo, sodalite, sapphire, blue aventurine	Geranium, jasmine, basil, lavender, rosemary	Purple foods – figs, raisins, eggplant, purple potatoes, prunes	Daydream, imagine the life you'd like to create, connect with your guides
7	Crown	Violet	Amethyst, selenite, clear quartz	Sandalwood, saffron, lotus, jasmine	Fasting - nourish with prayer and meditation	Connect with spirit through prayer or meditation

* Note that none of this information should be used to replace any medical, dietary, or mental health related treatments without the consent of your professional wellness care team.

Connecting With Your Chakra System

Below is a meditation to help you connect with your chakra system through observation, acknowledgement, and gratitude.

(Feel free to record yourself reciting this meditation and then listen to it as many times as you'd like.)

This meditation can be done sitting, laying down, or standing. Just be sure that whichever position you choose allows you to remain safe with your eyes closed or gaze lowered.

Begin by allowing your body to flex or stretch in any way that it needs. Maybe roll your head from side to side, perhaps forward and backward...Wiggle and stretch your fingers or toes... Roll your wrists in circles, maybe your shoulders, forwards and then backwards... Take a few moments to allow any physical energy to find release through subtle movement... when you are ready, settle into a position that you will find comfortable for the duration of the meditation.

Now I'll invite you to take a few deep breaths. Breathing in, nice and deep, expanding the lungs, the belly... and then exhaling out every last bit of air from your lungs. Breath in again, nice deep breath, again expanding the lungs, the belly, really filling yourself all the way up, and then exhaling out every last bit of air, feeling your navel draw in towards the spine, until you breathe in again, one last deep breath, expanding, filling, and then one final exhale through the mouth, letting it all go.

Now release any control of the breath and return to your natural breathing.

...continued

Connecting With Your Chakra System (cont.)

Take a moment to bring your attention to the base of your spine. Here at the base of the spine you see a red orb of energy. This is your root chakra. This is the chakra of survival, stability, grounding, security... it glows a vibrant red...some may see it as a wheel or a disc...some see it as an orb...how does yours present to you? Take a few minutes and get to know your root chakra... How big is it? Does it vibrate or spin? Are there any sounds coming from it? ... What does it want you to know? ... What does it need from you? ... Take a moment to say thank you to your root chakra, for all that it does to support you...

Move your attention up the body to just below your belly button, this is the area of the sacral chakra. The sacral chakra is a deep orange color, and is the chakra of femininity, sensuality, emotion... take a few moments to get to know your sacral chakra... is it glowing or pulsating? How big is it? Does it have a sound? If it helps you connect with your chakra you may place a hand on your body, just below the navel... What does your sacral chakra want you to know? ... What does it need from you to continue doing its job? ... Take a moment to say thank you to your sacral chakra, for all that it does to support you...

Moving your attention up the body, focus in at the base of the breast bone, at the site of the solar plexus. The solar plexus is a bright yellow, like a sun shining out from the center of the body. This is the chakra of the masculine, your self-confidence, your will power, they flow through here. Take a few moments to get to know your solar plexus chakra... how big is it? Is it glowing or pulsating? Is it a wheel, disc, or orb? Does it have a sound?... Is there something it would like you to know? ... What does it need from you to best support you? ... Take a moment to say thank you to your solar plexus chakra for all it does for you...

...continued

Connecting With Your Chakra System (cont.)

Move your attention up to the center of the chest. Again, if it is helpful you may place your hands in this area. At the center of the chest is the heart chakra, it glows a beautiful green color, though some may see it as pink. This is the chakra of love, familial love, community love, self-love… the chakra of compassion and giving, the chakra that binds our upper and lower halves together… take a moment to get to know this chakra… how big is it? What does it look like? Does it have a sound or texture?… What would it like you to know? … How can you best support it in caring for you? … Take a moment to thank your heart chakra for it does to support you…

Moving up into the throat area, here you will find the throat chakra glowing a brilliant turquoise or light blue. This is the chakra of self-expression, communication, and truth. Allow yourself to become familiar with this chakra… how big is it? Does it spin or pulsate? Does it have a sound?… What would it like you to know? … How can you best support it? … Take a moment to thank your throat chakra for all it does for you…

Allowing your focus to move upwards to your forehead, this is the location of the brow chakra, also known as the third eye. This chakra is a gorgeous indigo color and allows you see beyond what lies in front of you, beyond the physical and material world, to imagine what else there might be… take a few moments with this indigo beauty and get acquainted… is it pulsating or glowing? How big is it? Does it make a sound? … What would it like you to know? … How can you best support it? … Take a moment to thank your brow chakra for all it does to support you…

…continued

Connecting With Your Chakra System (cont.)

And finally, moving your attention up to the crown chakra, at the very top of your head, this is the chakra that connects you to spirit, to God, to your higher power… this chakra is a gorgeous violet color, though some may see it as a brilliant white. Allow yourself a few moments to connect with this chakra, to get to know it… is it a wheel, a disc, or an orb? Does it pulsate or spin? Does it have a sound or a texture? Is there anything is would like you to know? … How can you best support this chakra? … Take a moment and say thank you to this chakra for all it does to help support you…

Now in your mind's eye, imagine seeing all seven of your chakras at once, spinning or pulsating, in unison, in the same direction, going the same speed… knowing that these beautiful energetic gates are here to support and care for you, to help you create the best possible life for yourself, every, single day. See and feel the roots extending from the root chakra, down your legs, grounding you into the earth… Feel the warmth of the white light coming down from the heavens, into the crown chakra, and bathing your entire aura in its essence. Allow this feeling of grounding and of warmth to help you feel safe, cared for, loved…Take a moment and give gratitude to this amazing energetic system and the support it provides you….

Allowing the energy of this moment to stay present within you, begin to feel yourself back in your physical body. It may be helpful to wiggle your fingers and your toes, perhaps flex your body in one way or another. And as you begin to move, remembering the energy that flow within you, around you, supporting you and caring for you.

When you are ready, and only when you are ready, I invite you to open your eyes.

Please take a few moments to reflect on your experience, and remember you can use words, images, colors, etc. Whatever best represents your experience!

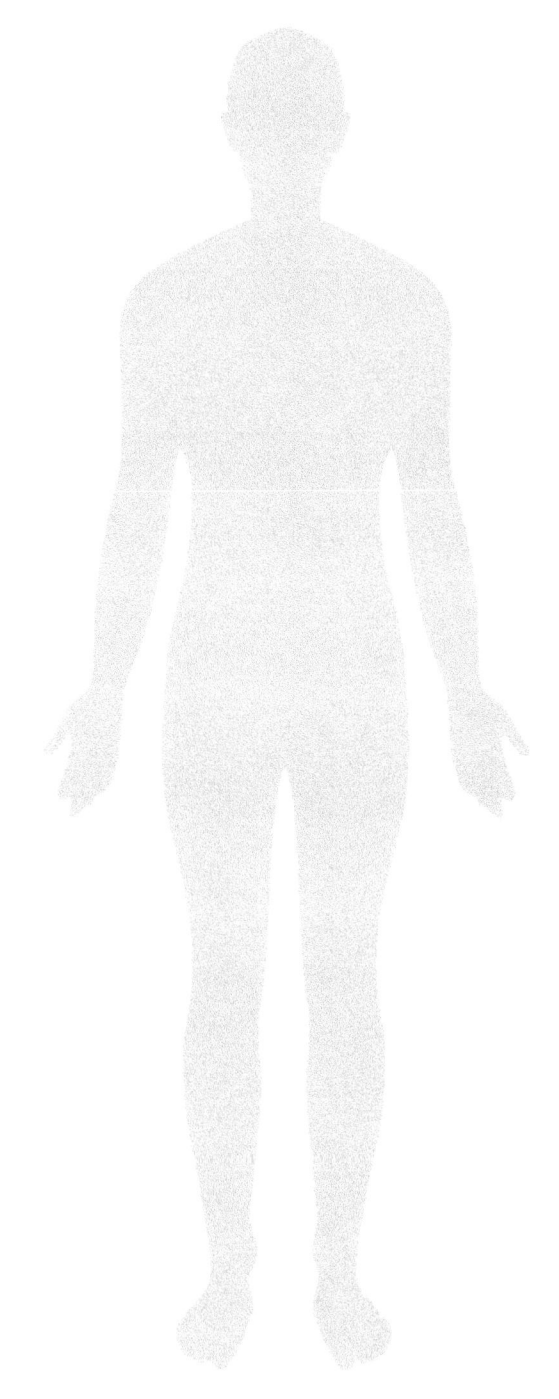

Make this body your own... add hair, shape, clothes... and then whatever you saw energetically during your meditation... your aura, chakras, anything else?

Chapter 2

What is Energy Healing?

As mentioned in the previous section, we all have a special life force energy that flows within us. This energy known as Chi, Ki, or Prana, flows through us like a river, ensuring that our energy doesn't become stagnant, or still.

Unfortunately, life isn't always easy, and it's a given that we will experience different injuries, either physical, mental, or emotional, throughout our lifetimes. These injuries create what are known as energetic blocks, the boulders in the river of life force energy.

Energetic blocks negatively impact our well-being by restricting the flow of our life force energy. Depending on the severity of the injury, and the length of time we endure its affects, our life force energy may be reduced to a trickle, or in some cases, these energetic blocks can be large enough to completely stop the flow.

When the flow of our life force energy is interrupted, the way we interact with the world changes, it becomes distorted as our system tries to adjust to the interference. Over time if the blocks are not healed, we create new patterns of functioning, psychologically, emotionally, and physically, which only act to reinforce the block and continue to limit flow.

Energy healing works through focused intention to remove these blocks, so that our life force energy can flow freely again, allowing us to heal. Anyone can access energy healing, to help themselves or others, as we are all made up of energy and have the power of intention available to us. However, depending on your current energetic state, working with your own energy may cause more harm than good, and over time using your own energy to heal can be exhausting.

To avoid wearing yourself out by using your own energy, there are several other forms of energy healing available which allow you to work with source energy, rather than your own. Through use of some of these other types, such as Reiki, you have the ability to help yourself and others without becoming depleted.

Reiki Energy Healing

Reiki energy is a specific form of energy, considered to be a direct connection to the source of life force energy. Out of the different types of energy healing available, the International Center of Reiki Training (ICRT) believes Reiki to be of the highest frequency and to be guided by spiritual consciousness.

Reiki originated in Japan, discovered by Usui Sensei on Mt. Kumara in 1922. Usui Sensei had several clinics and trained over 2,000 students, receiving an award from the Japanese government for the healing work he did after the devastating earthquake in 1923. Reiki was brought to the west by Mrs. Takata in 1937 but did not gain in popularity until the 1970s due in part to the stigma attached to anything considered Japanese after World War II.

When working with Reiki energy you are connected to the source of life force energy, a spiritually guided energy which when invited, will remove any blocks that may be present in yourself or others. Reiki Practitioners do not heal, but rather act as a channel for the Reiki energy, allowing it to flow through them to another. Because of this, the Reiki Practitioner's own energies will never be depleted, but rather, they will be continually refreshed as the Practitioner receives a session every time they give one.

As Reiki is guided by spiritual consciousness it will never do any harm and will never go against anyone's will. Reiki energy will always act in a way that is in the best interest of the person receiving the Reiki energy.

Reiki Masters & Attunements

People often wonder why an attunement is necessary. Because if we all have access to life force energy, why can't we just kick it up a notch? Reach out directly? Why do we need a "Master"? Is Reiki a cult?!?! No, Reiki is not a cult. I promise.

And being a Reiki Master does not give you any authority over anyone else, it merely means that you have completed the required training and associated attunements, and that you can teach others to do the same.

Though we do all have access to life force energy, we only have access to it at a specific frequency. The frequency of Reiki energy is higher than our normal frequency, and each new level of Reiki connects the Practitioner to a higher level of energy.

The Reiki Master who is attuned to the higher frequencies channel them during the attunements, helping new Practitioners connect. The attunement process is like an introduction made by the Reiki Master, between the new Practitioner and the new frequency of Reiki Energy.

During the attunement process the new frequency of energy, led by spiritual consciousness, enters the student and makes necessary accommodations or adjustments in the new Practitioner's energetic body and consciousness, to allow the Practitioner the ability to channel Reiki energy. Some students report mystical experiences such as personal messages from guides and loved ones, visions, increased psychic abilities, past life experiences, and enhanced intuitive awareness. Others report merely the feeling of a gentle warm glow enveloping their body.

In a new Reiki Practitioner, there are often energetic blocks, unhealthy beliefs, or patterns of behavior that need to be released through a cleansing process. The cleansing process begins during the attunement and typically lasts 21 days (3 days for each of the 7 major chakras). This process may cause physical symptoms such as a headache, stomachache, or tiredness as toxins are cleared from the body. You may also experience temporary emotional or behavioral changes, such as increased joy or sadness, unexplained moodiness, changes in your energy levels, or interesting dreams, as the unhealthy beliefs and negative patterns are released. What is most important during this time is to be aware of your symptoms and give yourself the care you need, whether it is more rest and fluids, perhaps a shift to your schedule, dietary changes, or spending more time in quiet contemplation around your current way of life and any long-term changes that may need to take place. If at any time you feel the need to seek medical attention it is important that you do so.

Every attunement and cleansing experience is unique to the individual, fine-tuned by the spiritually guided energy to meet the needs of each new Reiki Practitioner. No experience is better than another, as each is uniquely crafted for the individual. Be careful not to let your expectations lead you astray. Trust that what is, is exactly what it should be.

The symbol for Reiki is in Japanese Kanji and depicts the heavens above, the earth below, and the human healer as the in between.

- Clouds/Heaven
- Human Healer (Mind - Body - Spirit)
- Earth
- Life Force Energy

Chapter 3

Energy Healing & its Uses

As a direct connection to source energy, there isn't much that Reiki can't be used for. Any time you would send an intention, thought, prayer, or blessing, you can send Reiki with it. Sure, you can use Reiki as part of an in-depth meditative practice or personal session, but it can also be used while you do something as simple as watering your plants.

Reiki can be used to clear energetic blockages in anyone or any "thing" that has life force energy flowing through it. That means YOU, your significant other, your kids, friends and family, pets and wild animals, your food, houseplants, forests, jungles, rivers, oceans, the WORLD! There really is no limit to what you can do with Reiki.

To create the basic foundation for your Reiki practice, you can simply start with one of the two versions of the self-sessions described in this book, maybe add in a little Reiki to charge some crystals to help create healthier habits and support intention setting. But know this is just the beginning…

Reiki is a very personal experience, and you will find your own unique way to work with this energy. I encourage you to practice what I share with you here, and then let it naturally adapt and progress on its own. After a while, you will find what works best for you and develop your own practice based on your unique energetic needs.

Working with Reiki

The techniques for working with Reiki are simple and require no special skills, anyone can work with Reiki! All it takes is an attunement and you will be able to access Reiki energy for the rest of your life.

To get Reiki to flow, all you have to do is ask it to do so. In the beginning it may help to have a code word or starting phrase like "Reiki Go!". I invite you to get creative and see what feels right.

While it is not necessary to be in a meditative state to practice Reiki, taking a few moments to focus and center yourself is suggested. You may begin by placing your hands in prayer position, in front of your body (also known as Gassho meditation). Take a few deep breaths and ask for guidance in setting your ego aside. As mentioned previously, you are a vessel for Reiki to flow through, and as such, it is important that you don't interfere by getting in the way. Source energy knows what is best, and if you let your ego take over you won't give source energy the space it needs to do the work that it knows needs to be done.

At this point you may also want to invite spirit guides, ancestors, or other healing entities to join you. I typically just call their name and ask that they support the healing that needs to take place. Remembering once again, that I am not in charge, but rather being given an opportunity to share and receive healing by practicing Reiki. For example I may say something like "Dear Archangel Michael, please hear me as I ask for your help in this Reiki healing session" or "Dear beings of the highest heavens, dear Jesus, dear Quan Yin, I invite you to join me in this Reiki healing session. Dear spirit guides, ancestors, and ascended masters of the highest frequencies, I invite you to join me in this Reiki healing session."

Now if you don't currently have any guides you work with, that is ok. It is up to you whether or not you would like to work with guides. Over time they may come to you as you develop your energy healing practice, or you may decide to seek them out. Either way, it will not change your ability to practice Reiki, it's just an additional element you may want to add to your practice.

Next, set the intention for your practice by mentally stating what it is you are asking to be healed. For example, you can say things like "I ask that this session provide me with the healing that is in my best interest", or "Please send my plants healing energy to help them grow healthy and strong", or "Please provide me with the healing that I need so that I can sleep well tonight". The wording doesn't have to be specific, so don't fuss over terminology. Just be sure to take the time and set your intention in whatever way feels best for you.

Next you will want to imagine your crown chakra opening up as wide as it can go and asking Reiki to begin flowing, "Reiki Go!". In your mind's eye, see the brilliant white light of Reiki energy flowing down from the heavens into your crown chakra, and flowing out through your heart and hands in a continuous stream of warm and loving energy.

Getting the Flow Going

1. Begin by placing your hands in prayer position (Gassho meditation).

2. Take a few deeps breaths.

3. Ask for guidance in setting your ego aside.

4. Invite any guides you would like to participate in the session.

5. Set your intentions.

6. Imagine your crown chakra opening up wide and ask for Reiki to flow.

7. With your mind's eye, see the brilliant white light of Reiki energy flowing into your crown chakra.

8. Concentrate of the continuous flow of Reiki into the crown chakra and down into the heart and hands.

FAQs About Working with Reiki

Q: What should it feel like?

It is different for everyone, but most people feel warmth in their palms, and some feel tingling. When you use Reiki on someone else an energetic resonance is created between your two energies and the warmth or tingling will feel different as you move across different areas of their body.

The sensation usually increases when energy flow is good, and decreases when flow is low or blocked, but that may not always be true. In the case of an excessive chakra, there will be more warmth/tingling and the sensation should decrease as you flow Reiki into the chakra.

Q: What if I don't feel anything?

That is perfectly OK. Remember that everyone's relationship with Reiki is unique and just because you don't feel it, doesn't mean it isn't working. Over time, as you work with Reiki more often and for longer periods of time you may begin to feel sensations in your hands, or you may not. You may feel an increased sense of intuition, you may not. Unfortunately, I am not in charge and can't tell you exactly what spirit has in mind for you.

One thing I can tell you for sure, is that for the few students I have had that didn't feel anything, the people they practiced on sure did! Out of the 100+ students I have had come through my classes I have never had someone lacking sensation in their hands give an unsuccessful session. I invite you to trust that you are exactly where you are supposed to be, and that whatever you experience is exactly as it should.

Q: Can I do Reiki anywhere?

Absolutely! However, the experience will be different as your environment changes. For example, you can give yourself Reiki in a quiet room, with low light, while relaxing music plays, and you lay quietly relaxing on couch or in bed, or you can give yourself Reiki while sitting at your desk at work. In both cases you will receive exactly what you need from Reiki energy, as long as you can focus enough to maintain the flow of Reiki. However, if the environment is too busy you may not be able to focus.

When giving Reiki to animals, plants, environments, and communities I would recommend finding a quiet place where you can concentrate on your healing intentions. But that doesn't mean that if you are out on a lake you can't ask for Reiki to flow and send some Reiki love into the waters around you, or if you are out on a walk maybe you take a moment to place your hands on a tree and share Reiki through a gentle touch. Use your imagination and be creative. See what feels good, what works, what doesn't, and then adjust your practice accordingly.

Q: How long should I do it for?

Depends on the situation. A self-session can be as long or as short as you'd like. Maybe you give yourself just a few minutes of Reiki before walking into an important meeting, or maybe you give yourself a 30min session every morning and evening. When it comes to self-session, I would say just go with what feels right, and at the end of the day if you aren't sure just follow the standard hand placements, staying in each one for a couple minutes.

When working with others, a standard Reiki session is about 50min: 10 up front to greet and check-in, 30min of Reiki, 10 minutes to wrap up, share any info you may have, and wish them well.

I have given 15 minute sessions at a healing fair, or done 90min sessions at a client's request. I would not recommend doing anything shorter or longer though, as one doesn't give you enough time to "get in the groove" and the other can be physically tiring.

Remember that when using Reiki energy you will never become depleted, as you receive a session every time you give one, but your physical body may become tired. Be mindful of how you hold your arms, bend your body, etc., and don't be afraid to use a chair or the wall to support yourself during a session.

Q: Can I spread my fingers, or do they have to stay together?

It is recommended that you keep your fingers together as a way to "cup" the energy coming out of the palm chakras but go ahead and try both and see how each feel. For me the energy feels dispersed, lessened, when I spread my fingers, so I like to keep them together, like in the image below. But maybe for you it will be different. Again, this is a unique experience for every individual, so play around with it and do what feels right.

Q: Can you heal physical injuries and illness with Reiki?

> Reiki energy can be helpful towards healing physical injuries and illnesses; however, it should never take the place of professional medical care for humans or animals. Reiki, like many other holistic practices, should be treated as complementary care, to be used in tandem with professional medical practices.

Q: Can I flow Reiki while I'm talking?

> Yes, but again, you may lose your focus which could cause the Reiki to stop flowing. The only times I have talked during a Reiki session is when I have worked with people suffering with Post-traumatic Stress or have a high level of anxiety about the session. Typically, I talk to them about what I am doing so that I maintain my focus, while increasing their level of comfort and familiarity.

Q: How many sessions does it take to clear an energetic block or heal someone?

> No way to know for sure. As a Reiki Practitioner you may have a sense of how long it might take based on your intuition but remember that YOU are NOT the one doing the healing, the Reiki is. It is important to remain humble and grateful for the opportunity to work with others in this way, and to be careful not to start believing it is YOU that is doing "the work". I recommend you be as honest as you can with yourself and the people you work with around any feelings you might have, but don't make any promises you can't keep.
>
> For example, when I work on someone and can *feel* an inconsistency in her energy towards the surface, maybe in the aura and away from the body, I can guess that it was caused by something recent and may not be

that big of a deal. After the session I might talk to her about it, tell her how it felt to me (something not quite right, a spot near the surface of her aura) and just say that it may be from something that happened recently that she is harboring negative feelings around. I don't ever make assumptions or tell someone that there is something "wrong" with them. I simply tell them about my experience and my thoughts about my experience. The rest is up to them.

Now if you are a therapist or other wellness professional, this would be a space that you could move into deeper conversation. As a coach, I typically do a 90min mixed Reiki/Coaching session with my clients. Again, get creative and see how you might be able to best use Reiki in your practice, and allow things to shift and develop over time.

Q: Will I pick up negative energy from people I work with?

As long as you keep your ego and YOUR energy out of it, you should be fine. When you work with Reiki energy, it is Reiki that interacts with the other person, not you. Now that being said, you will still be physically or energetically close to the person and it is possible to pick something up in your aura which will need to be cleansed.

To cleanse your aura **AT THE END OF EVERY SESSION** you will swipe your hands, still charged with Reiki, across your body diagonally in each direction, and down each arm (see the images below). This is traditionally called Kenyoku or Dry Bathing. You may also want to physically wash your hands with soap and water.

Kenyoku aka Dry Bathing

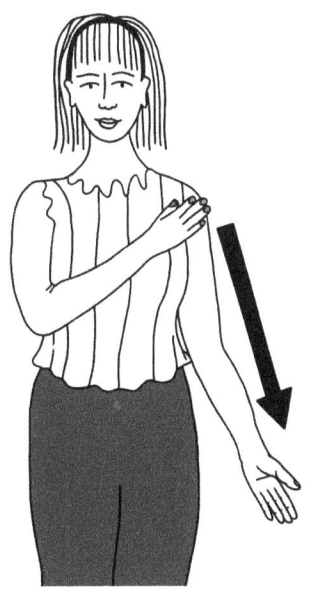

Self-Sessions

In this section I will share two different ways of giving yourself a Reiki session, the intuitive method and using standard hand placements. As I mentioned above, these methods are merely a foundation, and if you are guided to practice in a way that is different than either of these methods, please feel free to do so.

Self-sessions are a wonderful way to incorporate self-care in your daily routine. By practicing Reiki daily, you are able to reap the preventative benefits of Reiki as well as the reactive, such as a stronger immune system, enhanced intuition, a calmer central nervous system, increased energy, improved concentration, better sleep, and more.

I recommend a self-session twice a day, once in the morning and again when you get home or before bed. Self-sessions can get you ready for the day ahead, by wrapping you in a sort of energetic armor, allowing anything not meant for you to bounce right off. It can also act as an energetic detox at the end of the day, helping you clean away anything you may have energetically picked up or experienced throughout your daily interactions and activities.

Intuitive Self-Session

This is my typical go-to for self-sessions. Though I often incorporate a lot of the standard positions in my intuitive session, I do them in the order that feels right to me, versus the order they are listed.

I begin my intuitive sessions as I would any session, hands in prayer position, asking to set my ego aside, inviting my guides to assist in my healing, and asking Reiki to flow. I then raise my hands to my third eye and ask for guidance so that I may support Reiki in sending me the healing that is in my best interest.

I then move my hands to wherever I feel guided to do so and leave them in that position until I feel guided to change.

Standard Self-Session Hand Placements

The standard hand placements are a great place to start when giving yourself Reiki. They are also a great place to fall back to if you've had a hard day, you're tired, or your intuition just isn't cooperating.

You can follow along with the images on the following pages, giving each position between 1-3 minutes, longer if you'd like.

Hand placements for the head help us treat the Crown and Brow chakras. Individuals often report seeing swirling purple colors when working in this area and find these placements to be extremely helpful when they are feeling isolated, overly grounded, or intuitively stuck.

Hand placements at the neck and shoulders work with the energies of the Throat chakra.

There is often a lot of stress carried upon the shoulders, silently burdened, ignored and pushed aside.

The top hand placement works to help loosen the stress, to break up the mass into more manageable bits to be cleared away.

The bottom hand placement brings in the heart chakra and helps us remember we don't have to suffer in silence, and we are never alone.

This hand placement reminds us to love ourselves, to give ourselves a break. By working with the Heart chakra, we encourage self-compassion, remembering we're doing the best we can.

Heavy energies and emotions can often be found in the abdomen and groin areas, as they often house what we energetically avoid and push away.

In this space is the Solar Plexus, the Sacral, and the Root chakras. The hub of self-esteem, self-worth, sensuality, family, and safety.

Be gentle with yourself in this space. Try not to rush any work you do here, but rather be patient with what comes forward. And perhaps practice allowing that which is uncomfortable to surface and be set free.

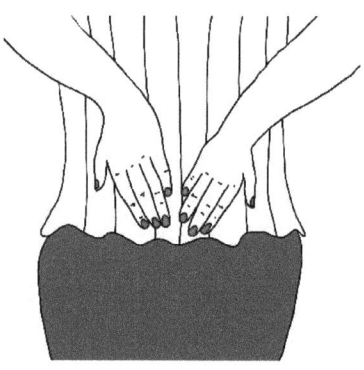

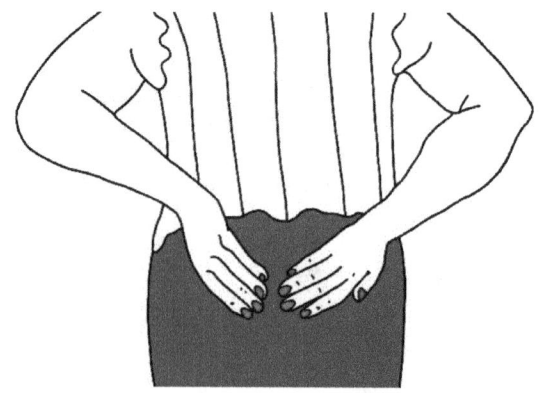

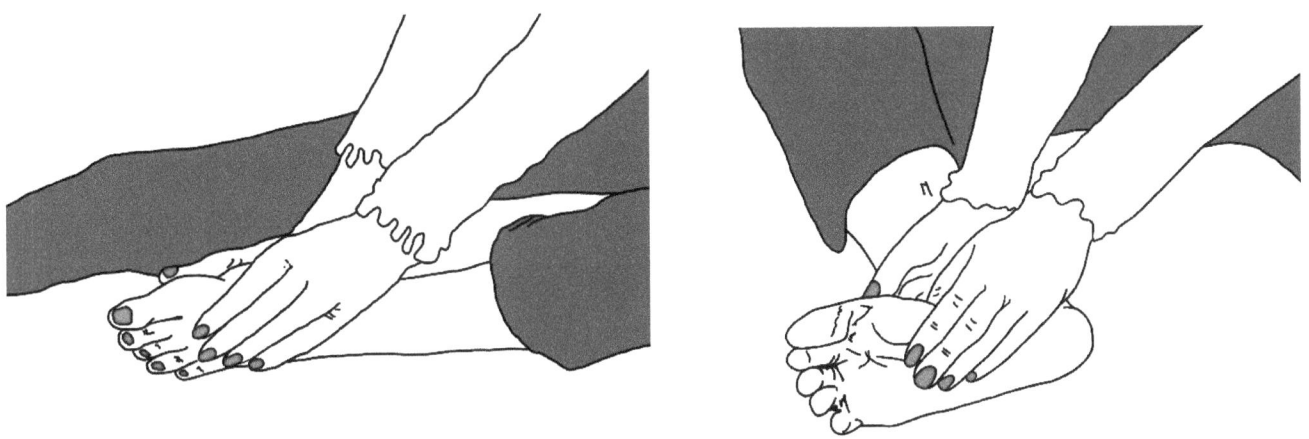

The feet are our primary source of grounding, and unfortunately moves through untold quantities of energetic junk each and every day.

They are one of the most important parts of body, and yet they are often the most overworked and under cared for.

Give the feet the time they deserve so they may continue to allow a strong connection to the grounding energies of Earth, which help to keep you safe, healthy, and strong.

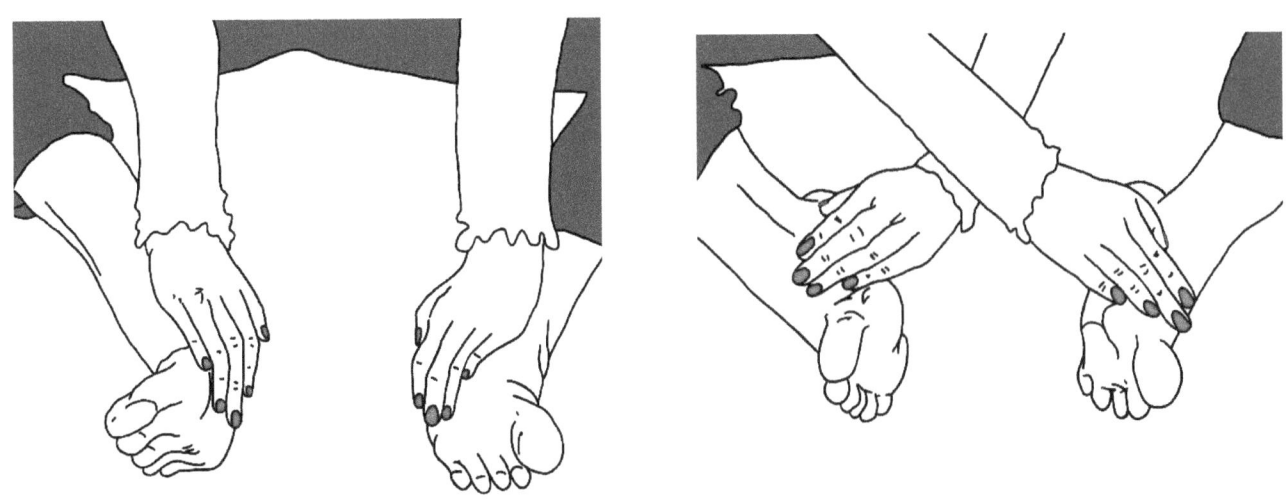

Alternative Sessions and Hand Placements

In addition to the methods discussed above, some Practitioners (including myself) experience greater sensation when they hover above the physical body approximately 2-4 inches. I highly suggest you try both, give a session touching and give one without, see which feels best to you.

There may also be times that you can't physically reach the part of your body you would like to give Reiki to. If that happens you can simply beam Reiki at the intended body part, confident the Reiki energy understands your intentions and will respond in a way that serves your best interest.

Beaming Reiki also works well when you are sending Reiki energy to an object or being in the distance, working with animals, or when you are sending Reiki to a situation or something more general in nature.

Now Let's Practice...
With a Guided Intuitive Self-Session Meditation

One the next page is a meditation to lead you into an intuitive self-session. This meditation will help you begin to tune in to your energetic body and identify any blocks that may be present.

Feel free to record yourself reciting this meditation and listen to it as many times as you'd like. At the end of the meditation, you are left to continue giving yourself Reiki as you are guided to do so. There is no specific time limit, you may take 5 minutes or 45 minutes, simply give yourself what you need, or what you have time for!

When I complete intuitive self-session of this style I often zone out, so to help bring me back to the real world, I often set a timer with a gentle tone on my phone.

...continued

Guided Intuitive Self-Session Meditation (cont.)

Begin by finding a comfortable sitting position, one that will allow you to move your hands and arms freely. Once you have found your seat, I invite you to place your hands in prayer position. Ask that your ego be set aside, and if it is in your practice, feel free to take a moment and invite any guides you would like to help participate in this healing session.

The intention for this session is to heal whatever is in your best interest at this time. Take a moment and mentally state this intention to yourself, asking for whatever healing in in your best interest at this time.

Now, imagine your crown chakra opening up wide and ask for Reiki to flow. With your mind's eye, see the brilliant white light of Reiki energy flowing down into your crown chakra, down through the brow, the throat, into the heart and out of the hands. Concentrate for a few moments on the continuous flow of Reiki… into the crown chakra… and down into the heart and hands… into the crown chakra… and down into the heart and hands… into the crown chakra… and down into the heart and hands.

...continued

Guided Intuitive Self-Session Meditation (cont.)

When you are ready, and only when you are ready, raise your hands, still pressed together, to just in front of your third eye. Ask for Reiki to guide your hands to where you need healing energy to flow. Remember to breathe, and be patient.

Focusing on the flow of energy, down into the crown chakra… and down into the heart and hands… into the crown chakra… and down into the heart and hands…
As you feel guided to do so, move your hands to the place where Reiki wants to flow the most. Place your hands in this area and allow Reiki energy to flow from your hands to this part of your body. Remembering to keep your fingers together, and allowing yourself to either touch or hover just a few inches above the area, whatever feels best for you, but still focusing on the energy coming down into the crown chakra… and down into the heart and hands… and out into your energetic body… down into the crown chakra… and down into the heart and hands… and out into your energetic body…you may stay here for as long as you'd like, or as until you feel guided to flow Reiki in a different location.

Continue in this way until you feel you are finished or your timer goes off.

Take a few moments and reflect on your self-session...

I encourage journaling after any Reiki self-session, as it helps anchor any healing energies here in the physical plane and can act as a reminder of things that may have come forward from beyond the conscious mind.

Remember that reflections can be anything you feel, and don't have to make sense to anyone, not even you. Written journal entries, images, or even just colors and shapes can all be helpful as we try to capture our experiences. Sometimes it is the simple lines that lead us to the greater discoveries down the road. It is up to you, use the space in your journal as you choose.

_____

_____

_____

_____

_____

_____

_____

_____

_____

Chapter 4

"In a crystal we have clear evidence of the existence of a formative life principle, and though we cannot understand the life of a crystal, it is nonetheless a living being."

~ Nikola Tesla ~

The Healing Power of Crystals

Crystals hold two types of power, innate power and assigned power. Their innate power stems from their geophysical properties and does not shift or change based on location, culture, or use. Their assigned power, however, is not necessarily static, and may change depending on who is using it and how.

For example, rose quartz has similar physical properties to clear quartz, which allows it to absorb and store energy, as well as any intentions associated with it.

Over the years, starting as far back as 7000 BC, rose quartz has been used as a form of jewelry or talisman. Romans used it as a seal of ownership, Egyptians believed it could prevent aging, and the early civilizations of the Americas believed it to be a "love stone", which is primarily what is us known for now.

As each of these civilizations attached their own specific meanings to rose quartz, they also energetically assigned the type of power it would emit. These power assignments are reinforced through cultural beliefs, and over time become a part of the energetic makeup of the stone.

This day and age, rose quartz is still commonly known as a "love stone", one that is related to the energies of the heart chakra, including compassion and self-love. If you meditate with rose quartz you can sense these energies, because they have been reinforced through belief and intention over thousands of years.

Now, all that being said... there are those who believe that stones come out of the earth with a set purpose ascribed to them by source, as well as inherent metaphysical properties that we can all use for our benefit.

Personally, as a Lumerian Crystal Healer, I believe that crystals, stones, and rocks (all the same thing really, just in different forms) are all an extension of Mother Earth and can be treated as a type of sentient being with needs and wants, just like a plant might have. I create a relationship with all the stones I work with, and to get the most out of your experience with them, I encourage you to do the same.

So, when you go to choose a stone for a specific purpose, try to keep an open mind. I invite you to visit a shop that you feel good about being in (vibe is important!), flow some Reiki into your hands and let your hands hover over the different stones. See which ones you are guided to work with, take a few minutes to hold them, resonate with them, *talk* with them. Don't limit yourself to stones that some book told you to use, just go out there and say Hi, see who says Hi back.

Using Reiki with Crystals

Clear quartz is THE stone to use in energy healing. As mentioned above its physical properties allow it told absorb and store energy, then slowly emitting it over a sustained period of time. Basically it was *made* for the work.

When you charge a quartz crystal it will absorb the Reiki energy from your palms, as well as any intention you send along with the energy. For example, If you wanted to charge a stone to help you focus more throughout the day, you would begin flowing Reiki as you would for any session, and then state your intention, as you would with any session, and then hold the stone between your palms and flow Reiki directly into the stone.

Some people find it helpful to create a mantra that supports your intention that you can repeat as you flow Reiki into your stone. For this example, something like this might work, "I am focused and calm, I am focused and calm, I am focused and calm".

I recommend doing this for as long as you'd like, but no less than 2-3 minutes. The longer you charge the stone, the more energy it will store. And YES, size does matter, haha! The bigger the stone the greater the capacity for energy storage.

Creating Crystal "Healing Bundles"

The simplest way to use stones in conjunction with your Reiki practice is to create what I like to call "healing bundles". Healing bundles are a nifty way to keep your intentions in one place, and when carried with you, they act as a physical reminder and energetic reinforcer, keeping you aligned consciously and unconsciously with your goals. I often make them for myself and my loved ones, as well as my clients. Once they are made up you can put them a pocket, purse, glove compartment, backpack, or even under a pillow.

To create a healing bundle, determine who the healing is for, what intention you would like to send, and then spend some time choosing which stones you think would best support this intention. Sometimes I have stones on hand I like to "re-use" and sometimes I need to do a little shopping.

If you decide to use a stone that has been in use for a different reason, maybe it's going from one healing bundle to another, be sure to clean and clear that stone. You can do this by burying it in the dirt (usually for a couple days), give it a bath (be sure it can handle water, Selenite for example will dissolve), or use Reiki. To use Reiki to clear a stone you simply flow Reiki into the stone with the intention to clean and clear the stone. You just want to be sure that whatever energy you put into it previously has been cleared before you charge it with something new.

After you decide who the bag is for, what your intention is, and what stones you want to use, you need to put it all together! I always have a few little velvet or mesh bags on hand, but you really can use any kind of bag you'd like.

In a typical healing bundle, I will have one quartz crystal, two additional stones that support my intention, and a small piece of paper with my mantra/intention/affirmation written on it. Below is an example of a bag I have made in the past for someone experiencing low self-esteem.

To charge the bundle, you will begin to flow Reiki as you would for any other session, then place the bundle between your hands and repeat your mantra while flowing Reiki into the bundle. Continue to do this for a minimum of 2-3 minutes, and then you can give the bundle to the person, place it on your altar, or carry it with you. If you have access to it, it is a good idea to re-charge it daily as a part of your morning practice.

Creating a Healing Bundle

Clear Quartz to act as the primary crystal which will hold your Reiki energy and intention

Carnelian for courage. This stone was often worn on the armor of warriors in battle.

A note writing out the mantra to repeat while charging the stones

Sara, you are amazing and have the courage to achieve anything you put your mind to

Rose Quartz for Self-Love, Respect & Compassion

Chapter 5

A Medicine Woman's Prayer

I will not rescue you,
For you are not powerless.

I will not fix you,
For you are not broken.

I will not heal you,
For I see in you wholeness.

I will walk with you through
the darkness,
As you remember your light.

Tending to the Wellness of Others

First and foremost, it is an honor to be able to work with another person or living being in this way. It is important that you remember this. Any living being, human or animal, that allows you to work with them in this way has given you an incredible amount of trust, and it is imperative that you have the highest level of respect when working with them.

Every being you work with, particularly humans and animals, will have a different level of comfort when it comes to you being in their energetic and physical space. I find that it is best, especially the first time, to take the time to ask them about their experiences and expectations. This will help create an environment of trust and safety, helping you both to relax and for Reiki to flow more easily.

There may be times you encounter someone whose energy doesn't feel *safe* to you, someone who you just get a gut feeling about, someone that you don't want to work with. I want to very clearly tell you that you can say no. Trust your intuition and just say no, but politely. It doesn't necessarily mean they are a terrible person or anything like that, but rather, it could just be that you aren't the right person for them to work with, which means if you force it, you could be robbing them of the healing they need. Listen to your gut, do what *feels* right, and do it in a kind and thoughtful way.

To begin a session on another, I recommend having them lay face up, with a pillow for their head, and perhaps a pillow for under their knees. A soft blanket is also a nice touch, and one that is often appreciated. Ideally you will want to be able to move freely around their body and have them at a height where you won't have to bend over much. Adjustable height massage tables work great, but you can also give sessions to someone sitting in a chair, laying on a couch or bed, or even to a dog as they cuddle up with you on the floor. There is no right way to do it, just benefits and disadvantages to each choice. Just be mindful when making the choice to do a session; ask yourself where you can do it to be sure you'll have the kind of physical access and comfort you need.

Then you'll start just as you would a self-session, and then choose to employ intuitive or standard hand placements (images on following pages), or even a mix of both. Again, listening to your intuition and doing what *feels* right.

At the end of the session, which could last anywhere from 15 to 90 minutes, remember to clean your energy with Kenyoku (Dry Bathing), swiping with Reiki hands across your body diagonally in both directions, and then down each arm. When you are finished, gently wake them, inviting them to open their eyes, and then to take a moment to ground and reorient themselves in the room. Afterwards you may choose to chat with them about the session or not, your prerogative. And that's it!

*** A note about hands on sessions – they are not necessarily legal in every state. In many states to physically touch someone as a professional, you need a license like massage or physical therapy. Before practicing on others be sure to check your local laws and if you are not legally allowed to touch then simply hover your hands above their body and skip positions where that is not possible.

Standard hand placements for others

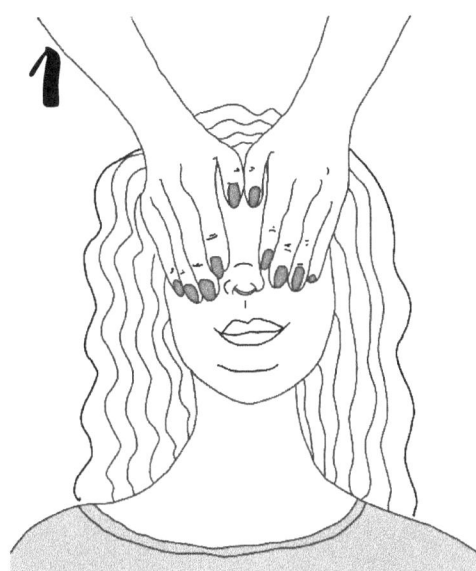

When placing your hands near someone's face, be sure they are clean and free of any scents.

Be mindful to cup your hands and to avoid placing any pressure against their face.

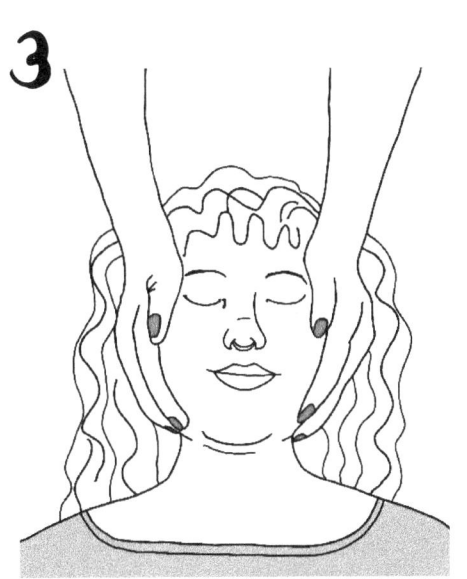

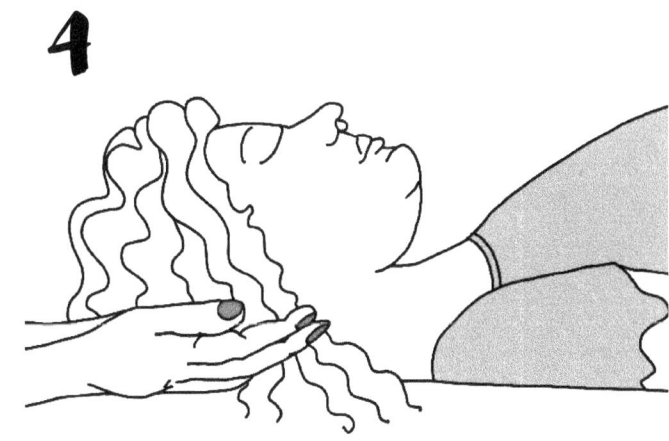

The neck and chest is a VERY sensitive area for many people. I recommend discussing comfort level around these areas before you begin your session.

NEVER put pressure on any part of the neck.

NEVER touch anyone's breasts.

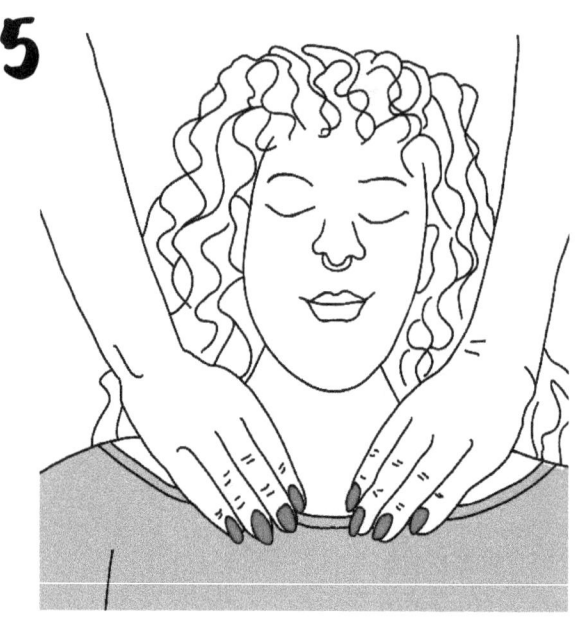

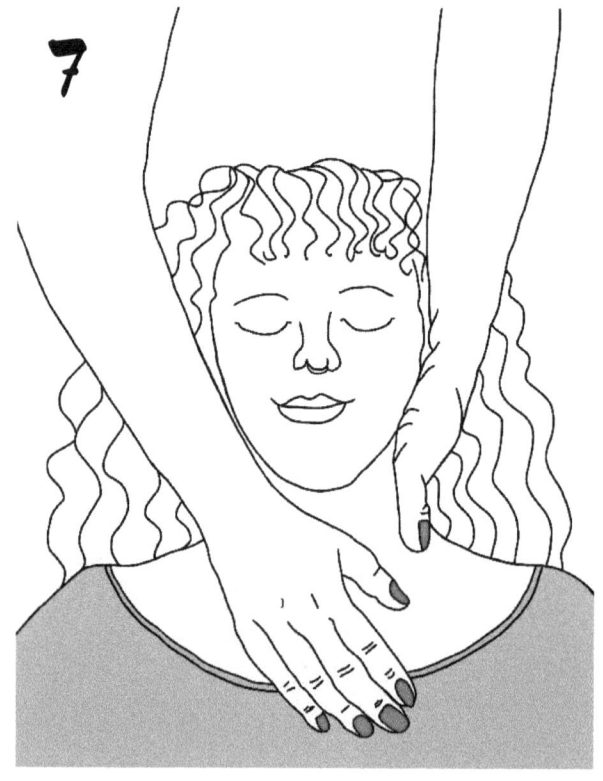

When working in the abdominal area, remember to keep your fingers together and to stack your hands like shown in the image below.

Again, be mindful of sensitive areas, and avoid any touch that may be considered sexual in nature.

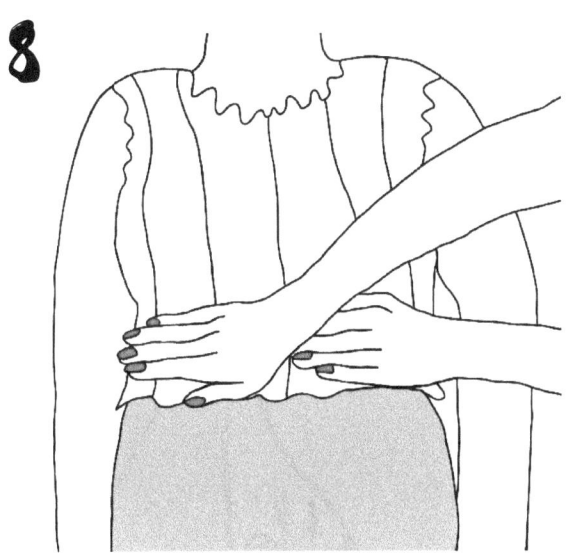

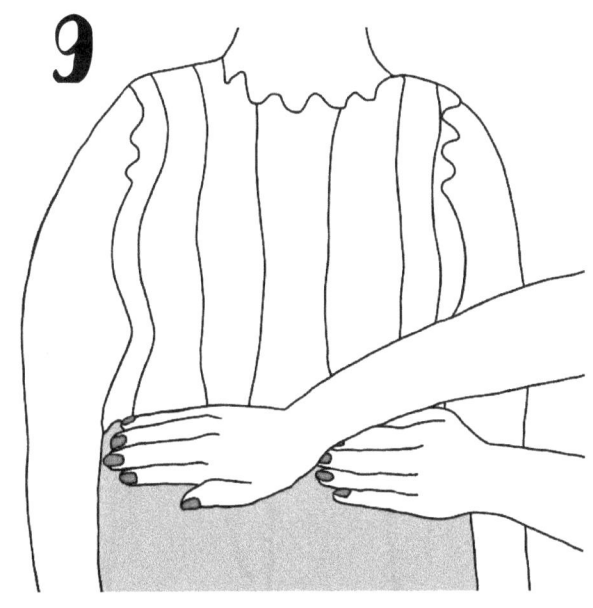

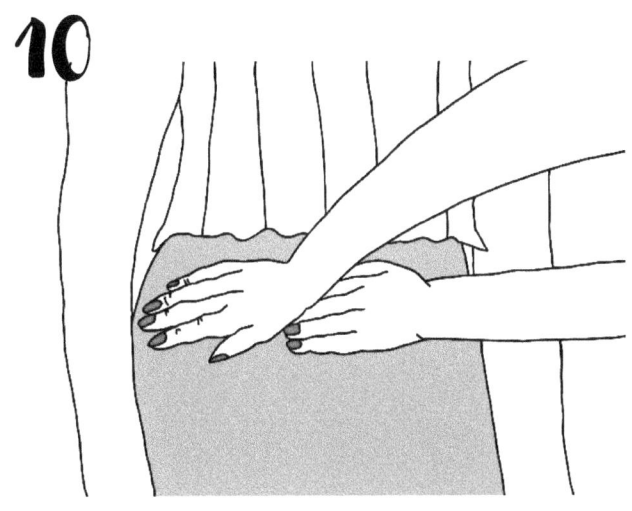

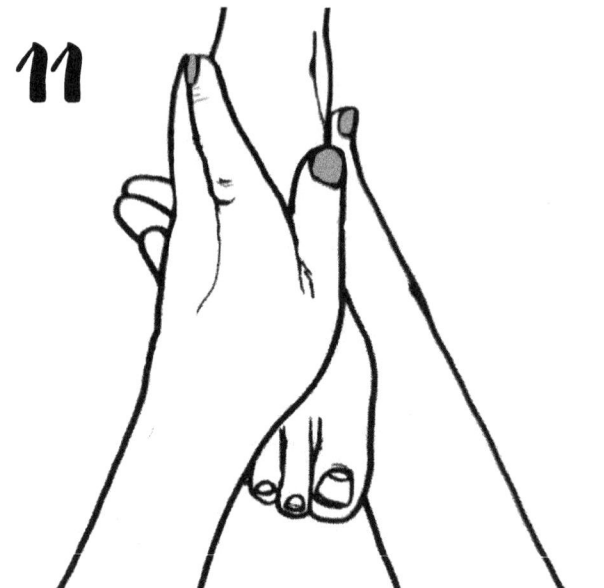

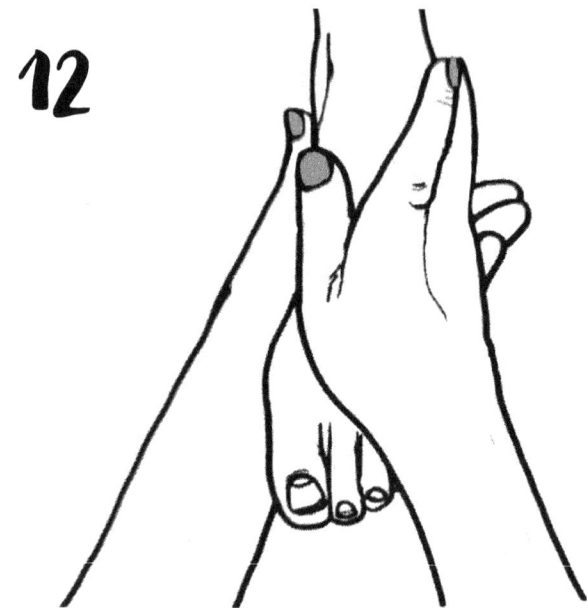

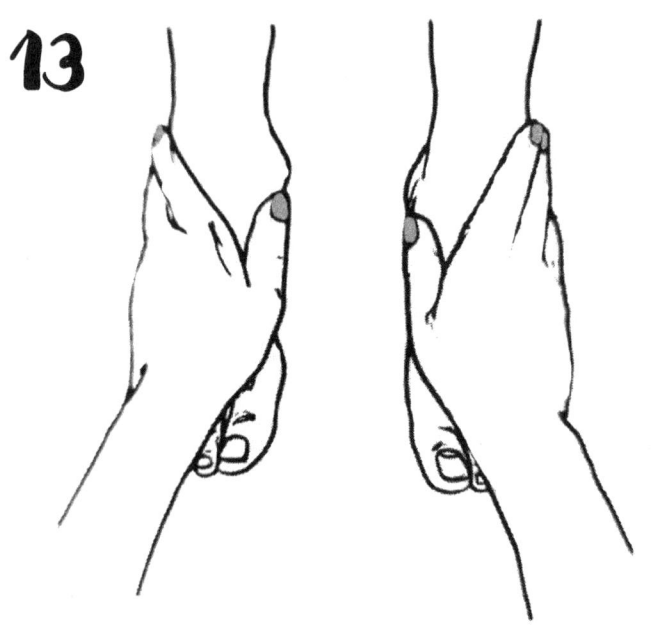

Remember…

The feet are our primary source of grounding, and also what moves through untold energetic junk each and every day.

They are one of the most important parts of body, and yet are most often overworked and under cared for.

Give the feet the time they deserve so they may continue to allow a strong connection to the grounding energies of Earth.

Intuitive Sessions for others

Begin these sessions as stated above, but instead of moving into standard hand placements, move your pressed hands up from your heart to your third eye and ask for guidance as you did during the intuitive self-session meditation. When you are ready place one hand above the head of the individual, establishing an energetic resonance, and then very slowly move your hand down along their body, taking time to notice any energetic shift, or guidance directing you towards a specific area.

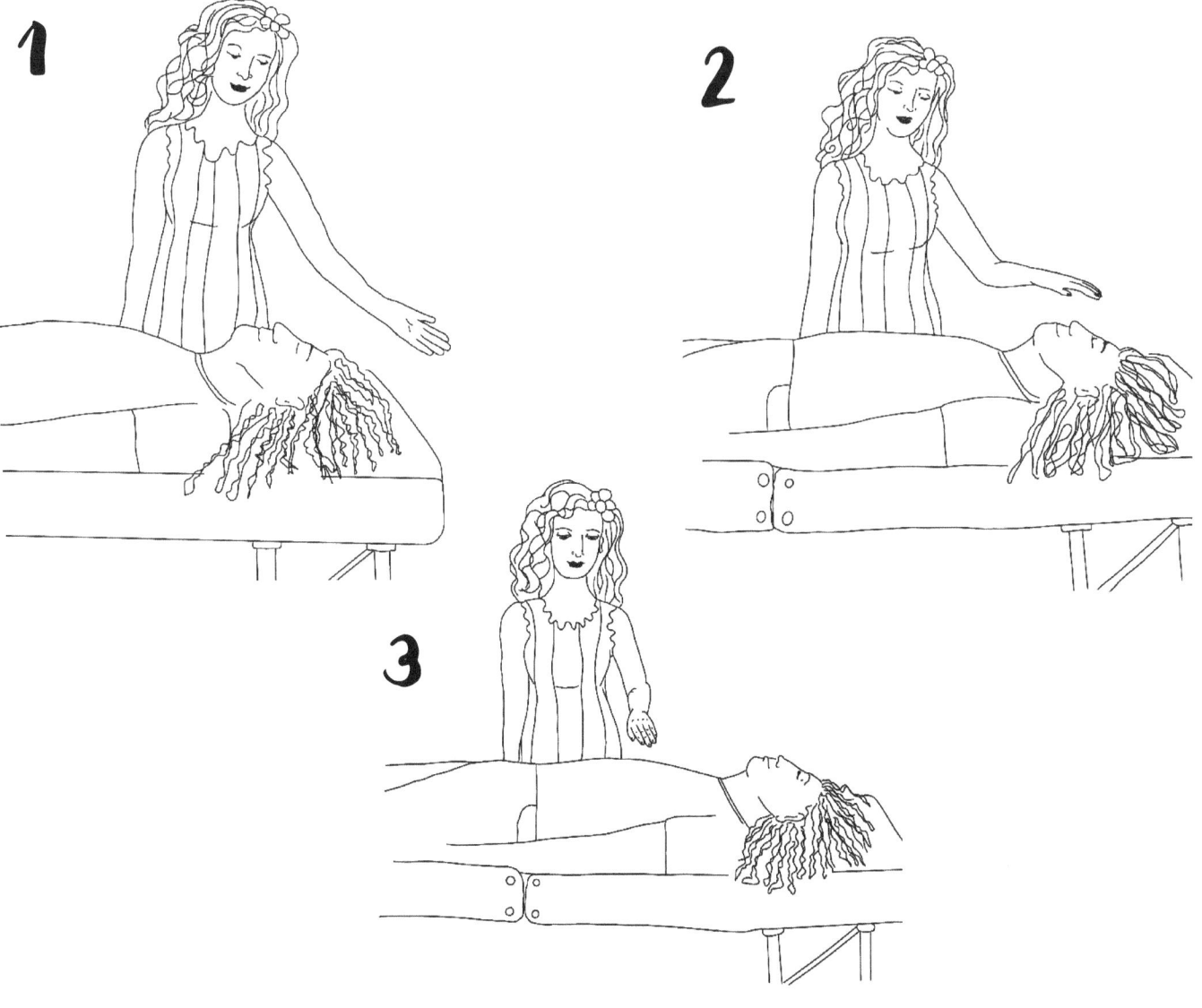

When you feel as though you have located one or more areas in need of Reiki energy, bring your hands together and flow Reiki into that area.

Stay in each spot for 3-5min, or longer if you are guided to do so.

You can also use this method to give a session that is focused on the energies of specific chakras. Starting at the crown and working your way down, letting your intuition guide you to the areas that need to most attention.

It is important that you move intentionally and methodically while working in someone's energy. Try to avoid "zooming" from one area to another, but rather take the time to feel into each area you are guided to work on.

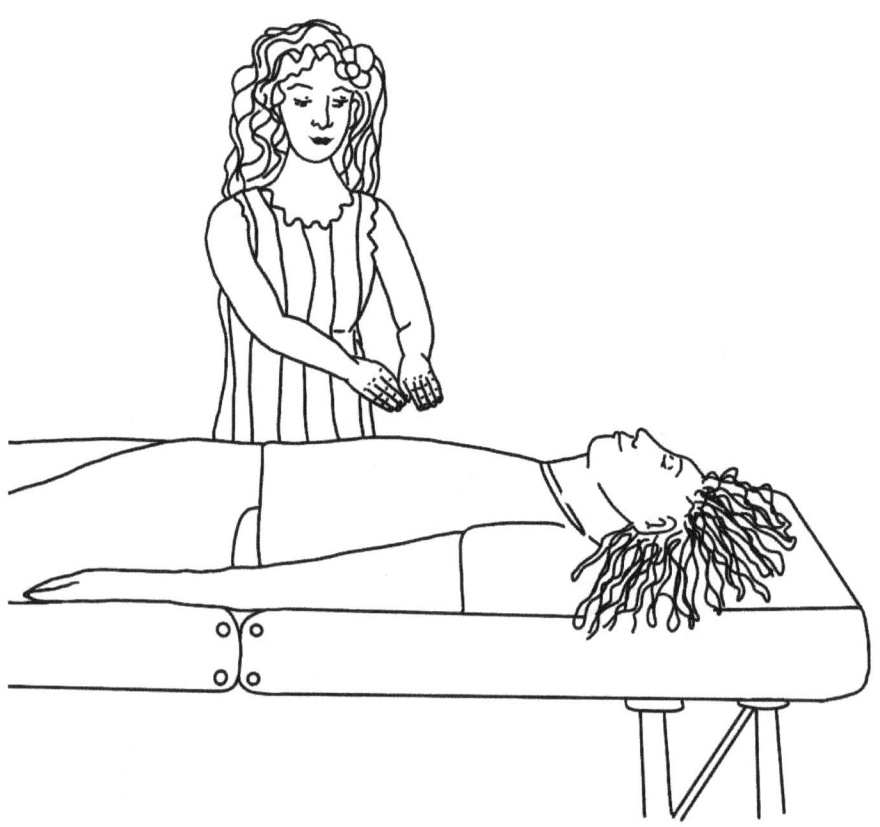

"The concept of total wellness recognizes that our every thought, word, and behavior affects our greater health and well-being. And we, in turn, are affected not only emotionally but also physically and spiritually."

~ Greg Anderson ~

Chapter 6

Using Reiki Symbols

So far you've been using Reiki without symbols, and as you move forward you may continue to do so, as they are not necessary to provide Reiki healing. However, the symbols that are given to you as part of your Level 2 Attunement are designed to focus your intention in specific ways, helping to guide the energy in a more direct fashion.

There are three symbols you will be empowered to use as a part of your Level 2 attunement; The Power Symbol, The Mental/Emotional Healing Symbol, and the Distance Reiki Symbol. Their true names are not mentioned in this book as a way to honor their sacredness. It is tradition that the symbols be kept confidential as a way to show respect for the power of the symbols, as well as to show consideration to others who have not been attuned and may try to use the symbols anyway, leading them to miss out on the true experience of Reiki.

Reiki symbols are transcendental, working not only with the conscious and unconscious mind, but also connecting directly to spiritual consciousness, communicating with the source of Reiki. When you apply the symbols during a Reiki session the energy will change to match the intention you set.

The symbols can be thought of as buttons, that when "pushed" activate the energy of that symbol. They are activated through your intention to use them, which is supported through drawing the symbols. There is no perfect way to draw the symbols, but I highly encourage you to learn to draw them exactly as they are presented to you so that you can connect with the energy of all the others around the world and across time that have used them before you.

When you are shown the symbols and given an attunement by a Reiki Master, an imprinting takes place that links the image the student has been shown to the metaphysical energies the symbol represents. This creates an unconscious connection deep within you that will support your conscious intentions. By memorizing the image of the symbol, you reinforce this unconscious connection, allowing the energies of the symbol to be present whenever it is thought of.

To activate a Reiki symbol you may draw it in the air in front of you, in front of or over another being, or in the palms of your hands before starting a session. It is best to draw the symbols with your whole hand, being sure to leave the palm chakra open with your fingers closed but extended. You can also activate a symbol by thinking its name, by saying it out loud, or by visualizing it. As a new Practitioner I recommend you draw the symbol with your hand until you get to a point where the image is memorized. Once the symbol has been "drawn" you will want to "push" it in THREE times, one for each element of the human healer; mind, body, and soul. And that's it!

The Power Symbol

The Power Symbol comes from Shintoism, and can be understood to mean "by decree of the divine", and is used in a way similar to Christians saying Amen or Pagans saying So Be It. In Reiki practice the Power Symbol is used to increase the power of Reiki, or to focus Reiki energy in a specific area.

Using the Power Symbol can clear negative energies and seal the space around a living being, a place, or an object, protecting you, your loved ones, or your belongings from both physical or psychic threat.

I encourage you to use it at the beginning of your session by drawing the symbol on each of your seven major chakras and in the palms of your hands to increase the Reiki energy right from the beginning.

The Mental & Emotional Healing Symbol

The origin of the Mental/Emotional Symbol is Sanskrit and means love and harmony. This symbol is one that works to create balance in all things through love. It is helpful for mental and emotional healing, relationship problems, bad habits or addictions, nervousness, fear, depression, anger, sadness, and more. The Mental/Emotional Symbol can be used anywhere there is an energetic imbalance.

The Distance Healing Symbol

The Distance Healing Symbol is derived from a Japanese spiritual saying and is composed of kanji characters. The name of the symbol means "The origin of all is pure consciousness". Pure consciousness exists deep within us, connecting us to the energetic fabric of the world around us. When we can connect to this place there is no where in time or space that we cannot reach. With the Distance Healing Symbol you can send Reiki across the room, across town, across the world, and even across time.

The most common use of this symbol is to provide distance healing sessions to others, but I invite you to explore its full range by working with energies you've identified as needing healing from past injuries. Now, unfortunately the Distance Healing Symbol can't erase past traumas, but it can ease the suffering and pain they caused.

You can also use the Distance Healing Symbol to create safety and protection in the future, by sending loving energy out ahead of where you will be going that day. As a teacher I have used the Distance Healing Symbol to clear and seal my classrooms before I enter them, and I have sent distant Reiki to students and members of meetings I will attend, always with the intention that all who are present feel heard and loved. You can also send it out into the world, to different crises or situations that could use more loving energy. There really is no limit to how you can use this symbol, so I invite you to get creative with it.

There are many different methods to working with the Distance Healing Symbol, no one is better than the other, as it really comes down to personal preference. I have listed several below, try them out over time and decide which one works best for you.

- Using a teddy bear or other stuffed animal, etc. to take the place of a body... You can lay the placeholder on a table, in a chair, wherever you would normally be giving reiki if they were there in person. Prepare like you would for a normal session but also draw the Distance Healing Symbol over the placeholder (pushing it in three times) with the intention to connect to the person who should receive the Reiki. Then perform a session on the placeholder as if it truly was the person. When you are done, seal the session as normal.

- Using a picture … when sending distance Reiki to a person or place you can use a picture to help you focus your intentions. Simply draw the Distance Healing Symbol over the picture, "push" it in three times, and flow Reiki from your joined hands towards the photo. You can also place the photo between your palms and flow Reiki into it that way.

- Using a piece of paper… take a piece of paper and write the name of the person or situation you want to send Reiki to, then figuratively draw the Distance Healing Symbol over the piece of paper and "push" it in three times. Similar to the photo, you can beam Reiki at the piece of paper or place it between your palms.

- Using visualization… this method takes a bit more work, but I find the results to be worth it. You begin by visualizing a gate, draw the Power Symbol and Distance Healing Symbol on the gate, "pushing" each in three times. Next you open and walk through the gate, across a bridge, to a room with a door. When you open the door, you will see the place you are meant to give Reiki in. It may be a treatment room with your intended recipient laying on a massage table, it may be a location from your past that you want to send Reiki energy to, it is whatever you decide it should be.

  You stay in this room until you are finished giving Reiki, and then you walk out of the room, close the door behind you, walk back across the bridge, through the gate, closing it behind you, then drawing the Power Symbol on the gate, pushing it in three times and saying to yourself with each "push", "I seal this session with Love and Light". Then you may open your eyes and feel yourself once again back in the present. I also find it helpful to repeat the symbol name to myself during this practice as a way to maintain focus and connection to *where* I am doing the work.

  One note of safety with this method… please do not intentionally put yourself into a traumatic memory or event without the presence and support of a professional.

Remember that these are all suggestions. Reiki is a very individual experience and it is imperative that you follow your guidance with how to best work with the energy. Try a few of these out and feel free to combine or edit the methods into whatever works best for you.

Chapter 7

Elements of a Complete Level II Reiki Session

Below is a step-by-step description of how to a complete Reiki II session. Know that this is the basics and you can add anything additional that is part of your unique practice.

1. Start with your hands in prayer position (Gassho meditation) and with your mind's eye, see your crown opening as you ask Reiki to flow.
2. Ask that your ego be set aside, set the intention for the healing to take place, and invite any guides you would like to have join you.
3. Draw the Power Symbol on each of your palms, on each of your seven major chakras, and once over your entire body, pushing each in 3x.
4. Start at the head of the person you are working with and begin your session by using standard hand placements, or allow your intuition to guide you to where healing is needed.
5. When it is time to end your session, seal the session by drawing the Power Symbol over the entire body of the person you are have been working with, pushing it in 3x. Then place one hand over the crown chakra and one over the root chakra, "push" down 3x, each time saying "I seal this session with love & light".
6. Bring your hands back to prayer position (Gassho meditation), give gratitude for the healing that has taken place for both you and the person you have been working with, as well as the opportunity to be a part of the healing process.
7. Finish by energetically cleaning yourself (Kenyoku – Dry Bathing)

Developing Your Own Style

As mentioned above, the steps I have laid out are simply the basics. The space you work in, the position you prefer to have the person in, and anything else you choose to add (crystals, sound, essential oils, etc.) is completely up to you!

One of the coolest things about Reiki practitioners (in my opinion anyhow!) is just how unique we all are. As Reiki is a direct connection to source, once we start working closely with that energy, our own individual gifts begin to blossom. Some find themselves drawn towards working with crystals, some towards sound healing, others find that their third eye or intuition increases exponentially… and sometimes it's all three or even more! There really is no limit to what you can do with Reiki energy or how you can use it as part of a beautifully crafted healing experience. Feel free to meditate, connect with Reiki energy, and see where it leads you.

Working with Animals

One of the questions I get asked a lot is whether or not animals can benefit from Reiki as well, and the answer is a resounding YES! I have personally used Reiki healing energy with my animals and those of friends for years and can vouch for the fact that most animals LOVE Reiki. However, it is important to remember, that just like with humans, they all might not be into it, and we need to respect that. Anytime we work with Reiki energy on people or animals we need to remember that a willing partnership must be created between all involved – you, them, and Reiki.

When giving a Reiki session to an animal, one of the first things you need to do, is build trust. If it is your animal and they are comfortable with you, you have a head start, but remember that animals are highly sensitive and we must introduce our furry friends to Reiki in a gentle and respectful way.

What I recommend is to begin flowing Reiki near the animal, not necessarily *on* the animal, to start. Respect their boundaries and allow them to control whether or not they get closer to you, and thereby closer to the Reiki.

In my experience with cats, they will typically move in and out of my "Reiki field" as they see fit, while I just sit and hold the flow constant. Though I have also had cats curl right up in my lap as well. Leave it up to them to decide, and trust that they will receive the healing they are meant to. Dogs are typically more open to it, again, based on my experience, but I always start the same way, as an offering, letting them choose how close they want to get.

Horses also love Reiki, and though I personally do not have much experience working with them, many of my colleagues and friends have used Reiki with their horses for years, some of them building quite the business out of it as well! Many horse owners, as well as ranchers and farmers look to Reiki as a means of alternative healing for their animals. Just remember that the larger the animal, or the less domesticated they are, the more you need to be cautious for your own safety. Never go into any situation where your experience with the animal has made you feel less than safe.

In addition to sitting in a space with an animal or giving a hands-on session, you can also beam Reiki in their direction, or use the Distance Healing Symbol and send it that way. It really is up to your discretion for each situation, just do your best to keep both of you as comfortable, relaxed, and safe as possible… really, it's not any different than working with a human, just a little less conversation.

If you are interested in learning more about using Reiki with animals, I highly recommend the book *Animal Reiki* by Elizabeth Fulton and Kathleen Prasad. It goes into great detail about the best ways to work with many different kinds of animals, and has some really lovely stories which share their experiences as Animal Reiki Practitioners.

Additional Uses for Reiki

Below is a list of additional ways to work with Reiki energy in your own life, but remember this is just the beginning, there really is no limit to what you can do with it! So feel free to get creative and explore different areas of your life where Reiki energy could be applied.

- Using the Power Symbol to clear & bless your home, workspace, etc. Anywhere you typically spend time really.
  To do this in a room, simply begin flowing Reiki, place your dominant Reiki Hand palm out toward one of the walls, draw the Power Symbol on the wall with Reiki, "seeing" with your mind's eye the white light flow from top to bottom, corner to corner as you push it in and say the name of the Power symbol, three times. Then repeat with the remaining three walls, floor and ceiling. Once you have drawn the Power Symbol on four walls, the floor, and the ceiling, place your hands out in front of you, palms down, and (just like closing a session) press down and say "I Seal this room with Love and Light" three times.

- Plants – Plants LOVE Reiki!!! You can Reiki the water you give them, or give Reiki directly to your plants, their soil etc. I often will charge a few quartz crystals as well and put them into my plants' soil – it's like a energetic "drip" system for them.

- Blessing food & water – Anything you give to yourself or others for nourishment can be sprinkled with loving Reiki energy.

- Aura Clearing – I like to do this in the evenings to clear my aura of the day's events and interactions. Simply flow Reiki and run you hands through the space around your body, through your aura, with the intention to clear away anything that does not belong to you or is not in your highest good.

- Reiki your bedroom and pillow for a good night's rest.
- Reiki your bath water before settling in for a relaxing bath.
- Reiki your shampoo, toothpaste, vitamins, medications… anything you use on or put into your body, Reiki just adds a little more healing energy and love.
- Reiki your computer, phone, or any other electronic gadget to help it stay "balanced" and in good working order.
- Use the Mental/Emotional Symbol to increase your focus and attention when working on a project or studying.
- Use the Distance Healing Symbol to send Reiki to anyone who is going into surgery – Reiki can help them tolerate the surgery better and can help them heal more quickly.
- Use the Distance Healing Symbol to send Reiki to any meeting in the future that you may be nervous about.
- Use Reiki to support creating healthier habits & empower your goals through intention and meditation, or by adding a healing pouch as described earlier. You can also create and charge a Reiki grid as described below in the same way.

What are some of the ways you hope to start using Reiki in your life?

Creating Crystal Grids

Crystal grids are another great way to work with stones and energy healing. To create a simple crystal grid, you can start with 6, 9, or 12 quartz points and a center stone of your choosing. The size of the stones will determine how long the charge is held, but otherwise is unimportant.

The quartz points are the stones that will absorb, hold, and transmit the energy you infuse them with. The center stone should be a stone in alignment with your intentions. For example, in this image I have a light blue Angelite center stone, so this grid could be used to support throat chakra healing or to help me better connect with my higher self. The size of the center stone should align with the size of your quartz points.

Once the grid is charged it will continue to emit your intentions to the universe as long as it stays charged. How often you re-charge your grid will depend on the size of the stones and the length of your initial charging. I recommend checking in with it daily, perhaps as a part of your daily practice.

To Charge a Crystal Grid

1. Set up the stones on your grid like the one in the picture.

2. Take a moment to get your Reiki energy flowing and draw any symbols over the grid you would like, remembering to push each of them in three times.

3. Beginning at the center of the grid, use your whole hand, middle finger slightly lowered as a "pointer", to draw Reiki energy over the stones. Follow the pattern in the drawing beginning with #1.

4. As you trace Reiki energy over the stones, be sure to repeat you intention, as you are charging the stones with every pass.

5. Make a minimum of three rounds, and once complete, hold your hands over the grid (or draw a power symbol over the top of the grid), and repeat "I seal this grid with Love and Light" three times.

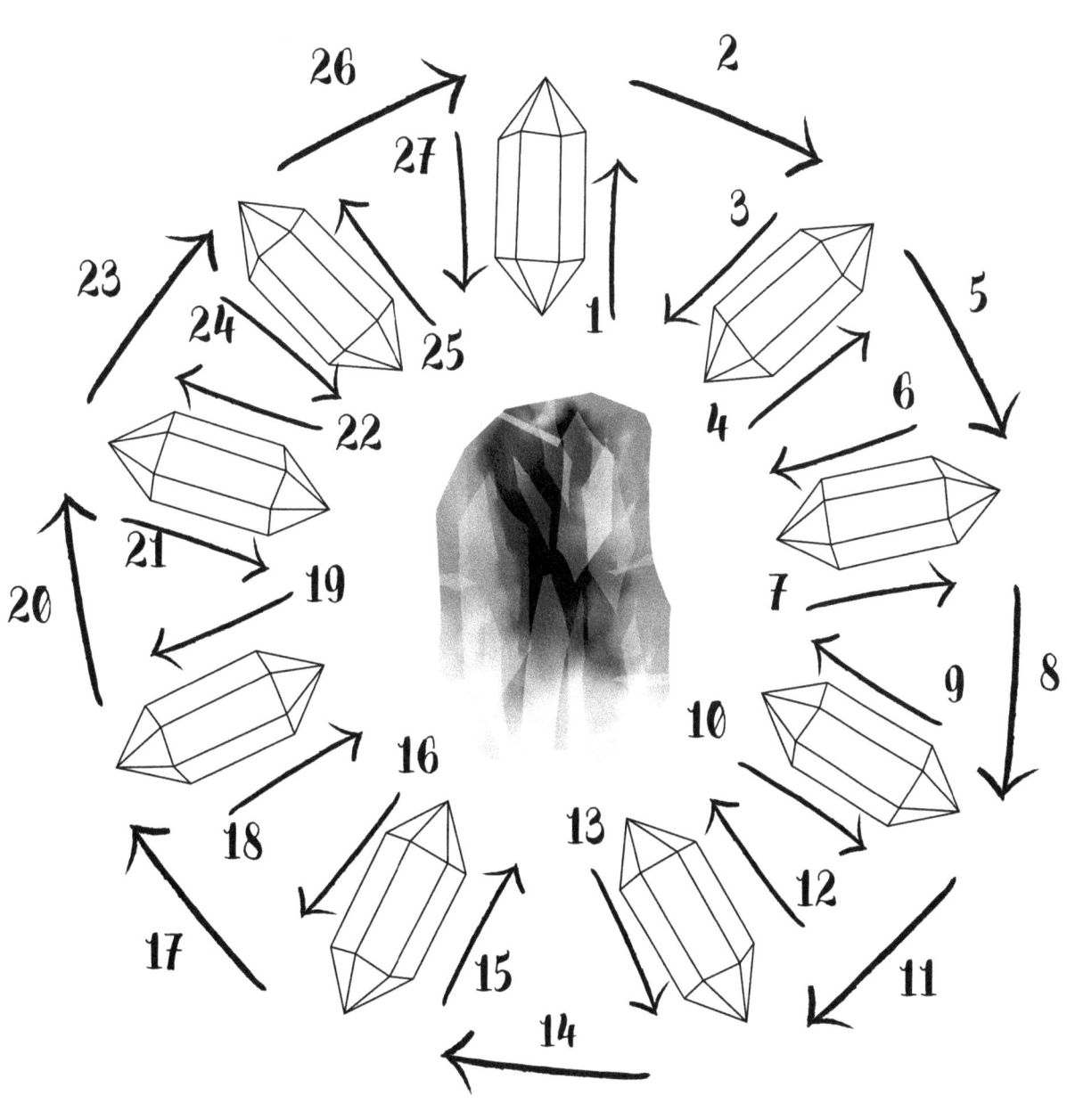

Using Reiki in Co-creation & Manifestation

Too often when we try to manifest our dream life we become overzealous with goals and commitments which end up harming us, instead of helping. Now, I'm not saying goals are a bad idea, but what I want you to consider is how limited your world view is. Spirit, the Universe, God, Goddess, whatever name you'd like to put on our higher power, just knows more, sees more, generally just has a wider view available. When we become overly focused on a specific way of being, of how things are supposed to go, we limit ourselves. The gifts that are intended for us can't be delivered if we aren't open to accepting them.

As you begin to work more with Reiki energy your intuition will become enhanced, your connection to the world around you will deepen, and the universe will begin to move things out of your way, widening your path. It is imperative that you relax the reigns and allow for some flexibility in what comes.

To stay open but still work towards manifesting the life of your dreams I want to offer you the option of asking for what is in *your highest good*. This may or may not include things you are already aware of, but it leaves room for the gifts that are coming.

You can still work towards eating healthier, being more compassionate, making more time to be with loved ones, even getting a better job, but I invite you to try and focus most of your energy on the why, not the how. Leave the heavy lifting of "how" things will work out up to the Universe.

Creating a daily affirmation or prayer is one of the most powerful ways to manifest what you want in life through co-creation with the Universe. Choose words that have a positive focus and that are simple to remember. Make them part of your everyday moments through a sticky note on the bathroom mirror, maybe one in the car, and even one on your desk at work. Play around with different options and ideas and see what resonates most with you. There is no wrong or right way, only the way that helps you the most.

To create the life you want, you need to first get clear about what that is. To manifest you need to LIVE the energy of the life you desire. When we create nothing but goals we put all our energy into what if and when. Focus on what living that life will feel like, what emotions will be present in your body, what sensations will you experience on a daily basis? Figure these things out and then do everything you can to experience them now… THIS will align your energy with the future you want. Because let's be honest, we don't want the big house, the fancy car, the perfect butt, the most wonderful partner… we want how these things make us feel.

Take a few moments to focus in on your future, the life you want to create, and the feelings you want to experience... How can Reiki help you achieve this? Take some time to journal about this on the following pages.

Chapter 8

Spiritual Practice as a Business?

People get certified in Reiki for many different reasons, and often those reasons shift and change over time. Personally, when I decided to get certified in Reiki I never planned to give it to anyone but myself, let alone teach or write this book! But here we are, 10 years later, 100s of clients and students later, and many pages into this book, ha! And I wouldn't have it any other way. Because of that I decided to add this section on starting a Reiki Business, just in case you end up there too.

But let's be honest for a minute… turning a very spiritual practice into a business can get a little tricky. Especially if your WHY is "helping people". Even trickier still when the people you want to help the most don't seem to be able to pay for that help. So what do you do?

I wish I had all the answers for you, but just like how you will create your own unique relationship with Reiki, you will also have to do the same when it comes to your relationship with Reiki as a business. The way I see it (feel free to take what you want from this and leave the rest!) helping professional deserve to be paid just like any other profession. And if this does become a profession for you, or maybe you are just adding Reiki to your already existing practice, you deserve to be paid for your time. Exactly how much and in what way is completely up to you, but please don't ever feel bad asking for compensation. It is a trap that too many of us get caught in. When our needs are left unfulfilled it makes it impossible for us to care for those around us. So please, take good care of yourself so that you can continue to care for others in the ways that fulfill you.

On top of all that, the business world can often seem cold and calculating. Business goals, and the image of success can be easily impressed upon us by others. When we bring our spirituality into business we can begin to lose our focus, our WHY, if we aren't careful. People can begin to look like numbers instead of the beautifully complex human beings we are honored to work with, and the manufactured need to make more money with this program or that can become overwhelming. If you find yourself in this place, it's ok, I ended up there too once, maybe twice if I am honest. What is important is that we refocus, again, on our why. Remember that you don't have to be a millionaire or work with 100s of clients to make a difference. Every smile matters, and every ounce of healing we bring to this world makes a difference. Find your WHY, work with a professional coach or mentor if necessary, and then stick to that. Let your WHY lead you in all things, and remember, you got Reiki too! Meditate, flow that loving energy, and see where it leads you.

There is a spiritual leader in Sedona that I really enjoy listening to, Michael Mirdad, and he has said many times that all we need to do each day is ask "How may I be of service?", and I love that. As long as we stay centered, grounded, connected to the ultimate WHY as we bring our spirituality into business, we'll be alllllright.

And I want to add just a short note on competition… there is none. I am not kidding. Not in this line of work. There are millions of healers and bazillions of people. We all find exactly who we are supposed to work with, and that is that. You need to believe this and really, truly hear me when I say it, there is no competition. The people you are meant to work with will find you. The universe will make sure of it. Sometimes they can get a little lost, so you might come across someone that you know isn't a good fit for you, LET THEM GO. Refer them out, help them along their path, but let them go. If it doesn't feel right for you, then it isn't, and that is ok. Connect with the other Reiki Practitioners and Masters in your community, get to know them and how they work, support each other. We are all here to add more love to the world and the best way to do that is through empowering each other's work. So don't worry if someone chooses a different practitioner or class, they weren't meant for you, trust that and wish them well. Your people will find you. This I know.

Charging for Sessions

Over the years I have worked my way up to what I currently charge and have added many other skillsets (Crystal Healer, Certified Professional Coach, PhD in Depth Psychology, etc.) to my sessions which contribute to the decisions I make around my fees. When I was a new Reiki Practitioner, I used a method recommended to me by my teacher to help get more comfortable in the work and ease into charging for my sessions; the first 10 sessions were only $20, the next 10 were $30, the 10 after that $40, and so on and so on, until I got to a price I was comfortable with. This helped me build experience without the pressure of a high price tag, and also take my time deciding what I was going to charge. I also did many swaps with people for things like haircuts, tattoos, produce, etc. It really is incredible what people are willing to swap if you just ask! Plus all of this helped me connect to my community and get the word out about who I was and what I was up to.

What I invite you to do when you start working on what to charge, is to reflect on the following questions…

1. What is my required income so that my needs are met?
2. Do I expect all of that to come from Reiki sessions? Or do I have other forms of income available?
3. How much went into my being able to provide the work I do? Cost of education, time spent in trainings, practicing, preparing, cost of tools, materials, space rental, etc. (Charge based on what you know and are capable of, not just how long the session is)
4. What is the going rate for what I offer in my area? How can I be competitive?
5. If I am struggling with charging or charging more, WHY? Do I have issues with money, accepting generosity, allowing abundance in my life? Or is there a different reason?

As you get going on this venture I also recommend working with a professional coach or mentor if you are finding yourself stuck somewhere. Just remember to choose someone who is in alignment with you WHY and your goals.

Tools of the Trade

Alright time for the nuts and bolts of the operation! The basics really are just a massage table, a blanket or sheet for the table, and maybe a bolster for under the knees (rolled up blanket works well too), and a pillow for the head. That's it! And you don't need to go buy a $3k massage table if you are just doing Reiki, we don't apply pressure to the body, so the requirements are different. I have purchased multiple tables over the years online for about $100, and I still have my very first table from 10 years ago! Still works great. Yes, buying a table is an investment, but it can also be a write-off, so keep that in mind.

Other things you can add if you'd like, are eye pillows, soft lighting, a nice speaker to play gentle music out of, crystals, singing bowls, etc. Really anything to enhance the comfort and relaxation of those you are working with are wonderful, but always just a bonus.

At the end of the day, you could give a wonderful session to someone sitting in a folding chair. None of this "stuff" is necessary to have a Reiki practice, they just make things a little bit nicer. The beautiful extras can also become expected based on who you choose to work with and how much you want to charge, so just keep that in mind. If you are offering a spa-like service and at the higher end of the price range for your area, your clients will probably expect a lot of the extra niceties, but if you are volunteering to give Reiki in a women's shelter or hospital a great chair session would make perfect sense. It's your practice, you get to decide. Just don't let not having all the perfect *things* get in your way. You have Reiki, and really that's all you need.

Finding a Practice Space

There are many places that a Reiki practitioner can practice, just like the tools you decide to use, it is up to the type of practice you want to create and the experience you want to provide. Many Reiki Practitioners work out of their home, especially if their practice isn't their main income. You can also look into renting space by the hour (some chiropractor offices, wellness centers, or metaphysical stores rent space), share a monthly rent with another wellness provider (like a massage therapist), or even travel to your client's location.

If you decide that Reiki is going to be how you make your full income, or part of a larger practice it may be best to consider a space of your own. A few things to consider are:

- Who are you sharing the office/building with? Being near other wellness professionals can have major advantages when it comes to referrals, as well understanding the need to maintain a relaxing environment.

- Pay attention to street noise and noise from any other business that is close. Check out the inside of your space multiple times throughout the day so you can get a good idea of the noise level. It is really challenging to provide a calm and relaxing environment when you share a wall with a restaurant dishwasher (yes, this happened to me, haha!).

- Cost of the space could be anywhere from $25/hr to $1000/month. Really consider your budget before you decide, because the pressure of needing to earn a certain amount to stay in that space can be challenging to deal with.

- Are you allowed to decorate in the way you want to? Will there be certain things (table, water cooler, etc.) that are shared?

- If you are sharing the space, be sure to ask what is expected of you as far as costs, cleanliness, etc.

Try not to rush into it, take your time and find the right space for you and your practice. Meditate with Reiki and ask for guidance, pay attention to synchronicities, and connect with your community for anything they might know of as open. And stay flexible… what you need at the beginning of your practice may be less that what you want for when your practice is in full swing. Allow yourself the time and space to build into that image.

Websites, Marketing, etc.

Many new business owners, whether Reiki Practitioners or something else, often get stuck right in the beginning because they feel like they need to have a website and business cards before they can do anything. That is absolutely not true. Over the years I can tell you that my biggest business feeder has always been word of mouth, and still is.

Sure, the website is helpful, and so are the business cards, just don't feel like you need to break the bank to get started. There are multiple low cost options available online for both, and many of them offer easy tools to help you design something that works for you.

But if you really want to market your business you have to meet people. I know many of us in the wellness industry are more of the introverted type, and that is ok. Some great ideas to get you started include:

- Having coffee/tea with wellness center owners (yoga studios, metaphysical stores, etc.) It can be less intimidating than just walking in and trying to have a conversation in their place of business, plus it gives you an opportunity to get to know each other and who knows, maybe they have been waiting for someone just like you!

- Have a booth at a wellness/holistic fair and offer 10 min chair session for $10ea.
- Look for local Reiki Shares and choose one to attend so you can get to know the other Reiki Practitioners in your area.
- Attend wellness-oriented events/classes in your area and introduce yourself to the other attendees.

Remember that not everyone you meet is going to be a friend or interested in what you have to offer, and that is OK. Again, those meant for you will find you, but for them to do that you might have to put yourself out there a little. Be gentle with yourself, only go where it feels right, and trust that things will align in your best interest.

Licenses, Taxes, & Insurance

Let me first say that I am in no way giving you legal or tax advice, this is merely a heads-up and a couple things to consider. Depending on the state or country you work in, the laws regarding business as a Reiki Practitioner can be different. I know that at this time (2023) in the United States Reiki is no licensed or regulated in any way, HOWEVER, most states have a law against hands on work with a client unless you are licensed to do so via another modality, e.g. Massage, Chiropractic, Yoga Therapy, etc. If you do not have a license to practice hands-on treatments, please be sure to check your local laws before you do so.

Other licenses you may need are for your business. Each state in the U.S. is different, as well as the county or city you may live in. Some make you register your business name no matter what, others only make you register a business name if you aren't using your actual name. Some counties may not require a business license, but the city you live in, that is within that county may... I know, it sounds a little nuts, haha, just make sure to check into everything legal and local to keep your business in good standing.

If it gets to be a bit much you can always work with a professional to help you get established. A good place to start is just call your local chamber of commerce or city office and ask for help getting started. You can also contact a local small business accountant who can usually point you in the right direction. It can be a lot, so don't get discouraged and just decide to go rouge! If you want write-offs, an income you can prove, and you know, to be a legally abiding citizen you just gotta do this stuff. You aren't alone, there are resources a plenty, just reach out to your small business community, and remember, even though this is spiritually based, it IS a business.

As mentioned above, one of the perks of keeping your business in good shape is the possibility of write-offs! In the past I have been able to write-off my additional trainings (e.g. Crystal Healing Certification, Yoga Teacher Training, etc.), supplies like essential oils, crystals, linens, tables, books, and more. If you travel to an event or attend holistic fairs you can usually write off those trips as well. So even if you aren't running a full-time business as a Reiki Practitioner, as long as you keep your business in good order and get solid advice from an accountant, you might be able to use it as a way to fund your spiritual development and growth as a practitioner.

Lastly, when it comes to legal stuff, is insurance. It isn't very expensive, around $100/year, and there are multiple options online for you to choose from. It provides peace of mind for you and shows those you choose to work with that you are serious about your business. It is also helpful to have, as many of the centers/studios where I have taught or holistic fairs I have had booths at, require it. Ultimately, it's up to you, but I do recommend it if you are going to be working with others in a professional capacity.

The Reiki Ideals

Just for today, I will let go of worry

Just for today, I will let go of anger

Just for today, I will thanks for my many blessings

Just for today, I will do my work honestly

Just for today, I will be kind to my neighbor and all living things